PESCATARIAN
COOKBOOK

MEGA BUNDLE – 7 Manuscripts in 1 – 300+ Pescatarian - friendly recipes for a balanced and healthy diet

TABLE OF CONTENTS

Introduction

Pescatarian recipes for personal enjoyment but also for family enjoyment. You will love them for sure for how easy it is to prepare them.

BREAKFAST

BANANA PANCAKES

Serves: **4**

Prep Time: **10** Minutes

Cook Time: **20** Minutes

Total Time: **30** Minutes

INGREDIENTS

- 1 cup whole wheat flour
- ¼ tsp baking soda
- ¼ tsp baking powder
- 1 cup mashed banana
- 2 eggs
- 1 cup milk

DIRECTIONS

1. In a bowl combine all ingredients together and mix well
2. In a skillet heat olive oil
3. Pour ¼ of the batter and cook each pancake for 1-2 minutes per side
4. When ready remove from heat and serve

Serves: **4**

Prep Time: **10** Minutes

Cook Time: **30** Minutes

Total Time: **40** Minutes

INGREDIENTS

- 1 cup whole wheat flour
- ¼ tsp baking soda
- ¼ tsp baking powder
- 1 cup pear
- 2 eggs
- 1 cup milk

DIRECTIONS

1. In a bowl combine all ingredients together and mix well
2. In a skillet heat olive oil
3. Pour ¼ of the batter and cook each pancake for 1-2 minutes per side
4. When ready remove from heat and serve

Serves: **4**

Prep Time: **10**   Minutes

Cook Time: **20**   Minutes

Total Time: **30**   Minutes

INGREDIENTS

- 1 cup whole wheat flour
- ¼ tsp baking soda
- ¼ tsp baking powder
- 1 cup cherries
- 2 eggs
- 1 cup milk

DIRECTIONS

1. In a bowl combine all ingredients together and mix well
2. In a skillet heat olive oil
3. Pour ¼ of the batter and cook each pancake for 1-2 minutes per side
4. When ready remove from heat and serve

Serves: **4**

Prep Time: **10** Minutes

Cook Time: **20** Minutes

Total Time: **30** Minutes

INGREDIENTS

- 1 cup whole wheat flour
- ¼ tsp baking soda
- ¼ tsp baking powder
- ½ cup raisins
- 2 eggs
- 1 cup milk

DIRECTIONS

1. In a bowl combine all ingredients together and mix well
2. In a skillet heat olive oil
3. Pour ¼ of the batter and cook each pancake for 1-2 minutes per side
4. When ready remove from heat and serve

Serves: **4**

Prep Time: **10** Minutes

Cook Time: **30** Minutes

Total Time: **40** Minutes

INGREDIENTS

- 1 cup whole wheat flour
- ¼ tsp baking soda
- ¼ tsp baking powder
- 2 eggs
- 1 cup milk
- ½ cup nuts

DIRECTIONS

1. In a bowl combine all ingredients together and mix well
2. In a skillet heat olive oil
3. Pour ¼ of the batter and cook each pancake for 1-2 minutes per side
4. When ready remove from heat and serve

GUAVA MUFFINS

Serves:	*8-12*
Prep Time:	*10* Minutes
Cook Time:	*20* Minutes
Total Time:	*30* Minutes

INGREDIENTS

- 2 eggs
- 1 tablespoon olive oil
- 1 cup milk
- 2 cups whole wheat flour
- 1 tsp baking soda
- ¼ tsp baking soda
- 1 cup guava
- 1 tsp cinnamon
- ¼ cup molasses

DIRECTIONS

1. In a bowl combine all wet ingredients
2. In another bowl combine all dry ingredients
3. Combine wet and dry ingredients together
4. Pour mixture into 8-12 prepared muffin cups, fill 2/3 of the cups
5. Bake for 18-20 minutes at 375 F, when ready remove and serve

POMEGRANATE MUFFINS

Serves: **8-12**

Prep Time: **10**   Minutes

Cook Time: **20**   Minutes

Total Time: **30**   Minutes

INGREDIENTS

- 2 eggs
- 1 tablespoon olive oil
- 1 cup milk
- 2 cups whole wheat flour
- 1 tsp baking soda
- ¼ tsp baking soda
- 1 tsp cinnamon
- 1 cup mashed pomegranate

DIRECTIONS

1. In a bowl combine all wet ingredients
2. In another bowl combine all dry ingredients
3. Combine wet and dry ingredients together
4. Pour mixture into 8-12 prepared muffin cups, fill 2/3 of the cups
5. Bake for 18-20 minutes at 375 F
6. When ready remove from the oven and serve

PAPAYA MUFFINS

Serves: *8-12*
Prep Time: *10*   Minutes

Cook Time: *20*   Minutes

Total Time: *30*   Minutes

INGREDIENTS

- 2 eggs
- 1 tablespoon olive oil
- 1 cup milk
- 2 cups whole wheat flour
- 1 tsp baking soda
- ¼ tsp baking soda
- 1 tsp cinnamon
- 1 cup papaya

DIRECTIONS

1. In a bowl combine all wet ingredients
2. In another bowl combine all dry ingredients
3. Combine wet and dry ingredients together
4. Pour mixture into 8-12 prepared muffin cups, fill 2/3 of the cups
5. Bake for 18-20 minutes at 375 F
6. When ready remove from the oven and serve

PEACH MUFFINS

Serves:	**8-12**
Prep Time:	**10** Minutes
Cook Time:	**20** Minutes
Total Time:	**30** Minutes

INGREDIENTS

- 2 eggs
- 1 tablespoon olive oil
- 1 cup milk
- 2 cups whole wheat flour
- 1 tsp baking soda
- ¼ tsp baking soda
- 1 tsp cinnamon
- 1 cup peach

DIRECTIONS

1. In a bowl combine all wet ingredients
2. In another bowl combine all dry ingredients
3. Combine wet and dry ingredients together
4. Pour mixture into 8-12 prepared muffin cups, fill 2/3 of the cups
5. Bake for 18-20 minutes at 375 F
6. When ready remove from the oven and serve

PLUM MUFFINS

Serves: **8-12**

Prep Time: **10**   Minutes

Cook Time: **20**   Minutes

Total Time: **30**   Minutes

INGREDIENTS

- 2 eggs
- 1 tablespoon olive oil
- 1 cup milk
- 2 cups whole wheat flour
- 1 tsp baking soda
- ¼ tsp baking soda
- 1 tsp cinnamon
- 1 cup plums

DIRECTIONS

1. In a bowl combine all wet ingredients
2. In another bowl combine all dry ingredients
3. Combine wet and dry ingredients together
4. Pour mixture into 8-12 prepared muffin cups, fill 2/3 of the cups
5. Bake for 18-20 minutes at 375 F
6. When ready remove from the oven and serve

SIMPLE MUFFINS

Serves: **8-12**

Prep Time: **10**   Minutes

Cook Time: **20**   Minutes

Total Time: **30**   Minutes

INGREDIENTS

- 2 eggs
- 1 tablespoon olive oil
- 1 cup milk
- 2 cups whole wheat flour
- 1 tsp baking soda
- ¼ tsp baking soda
- 1 tsp cinnamon

DIRECTIONS

1. In a bowl combine all wet ingredients
2. In another bowl combine all dry ingredients
3. Combine wet and dry ingredients together
4. Pour mixture into 8-12 prepared muffin cups, fill 2/3 of the cups
5. Bake for 18-20 minutes at 375 F
6. When ready remove from the oven and serve

OMELETTE

Serves: **1**
Prep Time: **5**   Minutes

Cook Time: **10**   Minutes

Total Time: **15**   Minutes

INGREDIENTS

- 2 eggs
- ¼ tsp salt
- ¼ tsp black pepper
- 1 tablespoon olive oil
- ¼ cup cheese
- ¼ tsp basil

DIRECTIONS

1. In a bowl combine all ingredients together and mix well
2. In a skillet heat olive oil and pour the egg mixture
3. Cook for 1-2 minutes per side
4. When ready remove omelette from the skillet and serve

ZUCCHINI OMELETTE

Serves: **1**
Prep Time: **5**   Minutes

Cook Time: **10**   Minutes

Total Time: **15**   Minutes

INGREDIENTS

- 2 eggs
- ¼ tsp salt
- ¼ tsp black pepper
- 1 tablespoon olive oil
- ¼ cup cheese
- ¼ tsp basil
- 1 cup zucchini

DIRECTIONS

1. In a bowl combine all ingredients together and mix well
2. In a skillet heat olive oil and pour the egg mixture
3. Cook for 1-2 minutes per side
4. When ready remove omelette from the skillet and serve

TOMATO OMELETTE

Serves: **1**

Prep Time: **5**   Minutes

Cook Time: **10**   Minutes

Total Time: **15**   Minutes

INGREDIENTS

- 2 eggs
- ¼ tsp salt
- ¼ tsp black pepper
- 1 tablespoon olive oil
- ¼ cup cheese
- ¼ tsp basil
- 1 cup red onion
- 1 tomato

DIRECTIONS

1. In a bowl combine all ingredients together and mix well
2. In a skillet heat olive oil and pour the egg mixture
3. Cook for 1-2 minutes per side
4. When ready remove omelette from the skillet and serve

RED BELL PEPPER OMELETTE

Serves: *1*
Prep Time: *5*   Minutes
Cook Time: *10* Minutes
Total Time: *15* Minutes

INGREDIENTS

- 2 eggs
- ¼ tsp salt
- ¼ tsp black pepper
- 1 tablespoon olive oil
- ¼ cup cheese
- ¼ tsp basil
- 1 cup red bell pepper

DIRECTIONS

1. In a bowl combine all ingredients together and mix well
2. In a skillet heat olive oil and pour the egg mixture
3. Cook for 1-2 minutes per side
4. When ready remove omelette from the skillet and serve

BROCCOLI OMELETTE

Serves: *1*

Prep Time: *5*   Minutes

Cook Time: *10* Minutes

Total Time: *15* Minutes

INGREDIENTS

- 2 eggs
- ¼ tsp salt
- ¼ tsp black pepper
- 1 tablespoon olive oil
- ¼ cup cheese
- ¼ tsp basil
- 1 cup braccoli

DIRECTIONS

1. In a bowl combine all ingredients together and mix well
2. In a skillet heat olive oil and pour the egg mixture
3. Cook for 1-2 minutes per side
4. When ready remove omelette from the skillet and serve

Serves: **2**

Prep Time: **5**   Minutes

Cook Time: **5**   Minutes

Total Time: ***10***   Minutes

INGREDIENTS

- 4 slices bread
- 1 avocado
- ¼ tsp red chili flakes
- ¼ tsp salt

DIRECTIONS

1. Toast the bread and set aside
2. Lay avocado slices on each bread slice
3. Sprinkle with red chili flakes and salt
4. Serve when ready

PUMPKIN FRENCH TOAST

Serves: **3**

Prep Time: **5**   Minutes

Cook Time: **15**   Minutes

Total Time: **20**   Minutes

INGREDIENTS

- ¼ cup milk
- 2 eggs
- ½ cup pumpkin puree
- 1 tablespoon pumpkin slice
- 6 bread slices

DIRECTIONS

1. In a bowl whisk all ingredients for the dipping
2. Dip the bread into the dipping and let it soak for 3-4 minutes
3. In a skillet heat olive oil and fry each slice for 2-3 minutes per side
4. When ready remove from the skillet and serve

COCONUT CHAI OATMEAL

Serves: 2

Prep Time: 5   Minutes

Cook Time: 15   Minutes

Total Time: 20   Minutes

INGREDIENTS

- ¼ cup oats
- ½ cup chia tea
- ¼ cup coconut milk
- 1 peach
- ¼ tsp coconut oil
- 1 tsp coconut flakes

DIRECTIONS

1. In a bowl combine together oats, coconut milk, chia tea and microwave until thickness
2. In a saucepan add peach slices and cook for 2-3 minutes
3. Place peaches over the oats and top with coconut flakes
4. Serve when ready

CACAO GRANOLA PARFAIT

Serves: **4**

Prep Time: **10** Minutes

Cook Time: **30** Minutes

Total Time: **40** Minutes

INGREDIENTS

- 4 oz. coconut yogurt
- ¼ cup gluten-free granola
- 1 tablespoon cacao nibs
- 1 oz. raspberries

DIRECTIONS

1. Place all ingredients in a bowl and mix well
2. Serve when ready

Serves: **1**
Prep Time: **5**   Minutes

Cook Time: **5**   Minutes

Total Time: **10** Minutes

INGREDIENTS

- 2 slices gluten-free toast
- 2 tablespoons peanut butter
- ¼ tsp flax seeds
- ¼ tsp chia seeds

DIRECTIONS

1. Place all ingredients in a bowl and mix well
2. Serve when ready

LUNCH

SIMPLE PIZZA RECIPE

Serves: *6-8*
Prep Time: *10*   Minutes

Cook Time: *15*   Minutes

Total Time: *25*   Minutes

INGREDIENTS

- 1 pizza crust
- ½ cup tomato sauce
- ¼ black pepper
- 1 cup pepperoni slices
- 1 cup mozzarella cheese
- 1 cup olives

DIRECTIONS

1. Spread tomato sauce on the pizza crust
2. Place all the toppings on the pizza crust
3. Bake the pizza at 425 F for 12-15 minutes
4. When ready remove pizza from the oven and serve

ZUCCHINI PIZZA

Serves: **6-8**

Prep Time: **10** Minutes

Cook Time: **15** Minutes

Total Time: **25** Minutes

INGREDIENTS

- 1 pizza crust
- ½ cup tomato sauce
- ¼ black pepper
- 1 cup zucchini slices
- 1 cup mozzarella cheese
- 1 cup olives

DIRECTIONS

1. Spread tomato sauce on the pizza crust
2. Place all the toppings on the pizza crust
3. Bake the pizza at 425 F for 12-15 minutes
4. When ready remove pizza from the oven and serve

RED ONION FRITATTA

Serves: **2**

Prep Time: **10** Minutes

Cook Time: **20** Minutes

Total Time: **30** Minutes

INGREDIENTS

- ½ lb. asparagus
- 1 tablespoon olive oil
- ½ red onion
- ¼ tsp salt
- 2 eggs
- 2 oz. cheddar cheese
- 1 garlic clove
- ¼ tsp dill

DIRECTIONS

1. In a bowl whisk eggs with salt and cheese
2. In a frying pan heat olive oil and pour egg mixture
3. Add remaining ingredients and mix well
4. Serve when ready

SPINACH FRITATTA

Serves: **2**
Prep Time: **10** Minutes

Cook Time: **20** Minutes

Total Time: **30** Minutes

INGREDIENTS

- ½ lb. spinach
- 1 tablespoon olive oil
- ½ red onion
- ¼ tsp salt
- 2 eggs
- 2 oz. cheddar cheese
- 1 garlic clove
- ¼ tsp dill

DIRECTIONS

1. In a bowl whisk eggs with salt and cheese
2. In a frying pan heat olive oil and pour egg mixture
3. Add remaining ingredients and mix well
4. Serve when ready

CHEESE FRITATTA

Serves: **2**

Prep Time: **10** Minutes

Cook Time: **20** Minutes

Total Time: **30** Minutes

INGREDIENTS

- 1 tablespoon olive oil
- ½ red onion
- ¼ tsp salt
- 2 eggs
- 1 cup cheddar cheese
- 1 garlic clove
- ¼ tsp dill

DIRECTIONS

1. In a bowl whisk eggs with salt and cheese
2. In a frying pan heat olive oil and pour egg mixture
3. Add remaining ingredients and mix well
4. Serve when ready

Serves: **2**

Prep Time: **10**   Minutes

Cook Time: **20**   Minutes

Total Time: **30**   Minutes

INGREDIENTS

- 1 cup rhubarb
- 1 tablespoon olive oil
- ½ red onion
- ¼ tsp salt
- 2 oz. parmesan cheese
- 1 garlic clove
- ¼ tsp dill

DIRECTIONS

1. In a bowl whisk eggs with salt and parmesan cheese
2. In a frying pan heat olive oil and pour egg mixture
3. Add remaining ingredients and mix well
4. Serve when ready

BROCCOLI FRITATTA

Serves: **2**
Prep Time: **10**   Minutes

Cook Time: **20**   Minutes

Total Time: **30**   Minutes

INGREDIENTS

- 1 cup broccoli
- 1 tablespoon olive oil
- ½ red onion
- 2 eggs
- ¼ tsp salt
- 2 oz. cheddar cheese
- 1 garlic clove
- ¼ tsp dill

DIRECTIONS

1. In a bowl whisk eggs with salt and cheese
2. In a frying pan heat olive oil and pour egg mixture
3. Add remaining ingredients and mix well
4. Serve when ready

TOMATO RISOTTO

Serves: **2**

Prep Time: **10**   Minutes

Cook Time: **25**   Minutes

Total Time: **35**   Minutes

INGREDIENTS

- 2-3 tablespoons olive oil
- 1 red onion
- 1 lb. vine-ripened tomatoes
- 1 lb. risotto rice
- 1 cup vegetable stock
- 1 cup cheese
- 2 oz. basil

DIRECTIONS

1. In a pan heat olive oil and sauté onion until soft
2. Place the tomatoes on a baking tray, drizzle olive oil and roast at 350 F for 18-20 minutes
3. Add the rice, stock to the pan and cook until rice is tender
4. Add the cheese, basil, tomatoes and serve when ready

SQUASH QUICHE

Serves: 2

Prep Time: *10*   Minutes

Cook Time: *50*   Minutes

Total Time: *60*   Minutes

INGREDIENTS

- 1 lb. butternut squash
- 3 tablespoons olive oil
- ¼ rolled pastry
- 2 eggs
- 200 ml double cream

DIRECTIONS

1. Roast the squash at 400 F for 18-20 minutes
2. Lay a baking paper on the pastry
3. Top with beans and bake for 12-15 minutes
4. Top the pastry with squash
5. Mix eggs, with double cream and pour over
6. Bake for another 20-25 minutes
7. When ready remove from the oven and serve

TOMATO TARTS

Serves: **2**

Prep Time: **10** Minutes

Cook Time: **35** Minutes

Total Time: **45** Minutes

INGREDIENTS

- 1 lb. pastry
- 2-3 tsp tomato paste
- 1 lb. tomatoes
- 1 tablespoons olive oil
- 1 tablespoon capers
- 1 lb. broccoli

DIRECTIONS

1. Unroll the pastry sheet and cut into rectangles
2. Spread tomato paste over each tart and drizzle olive oil
3. Scatter over capers
4. Bake at 400 F for 18-20 minutes
5. Meanwhile boil the broccoli for 12-15 minutes or until tender
6. When ready remove from the oven and serve with cooked broccoli

TOMATO AND ONION PASTA

Serves: **2**

Prep Time: **10** Minutes

Cook Time: **20** Minutes

Total Time: **30** Minutes

INGREDIENTS

- 1 tablespoon olive oil
- 1 onion
- ½ lb. penne pasta
- 2-3 garlic cloves
- 1 oz. parsley
- ½ lb. tomatoes
- ¼ lb. low fat sour cream

DIRECTIONS

1. Heat olive oil in a pan and sauté onion until soft
2. Add pasta, garlic, pasta and water to cover
3. Bring to a boil and simmer for 5-6 minutes
4. Add tomatoes and cook for another 4-5 minutes
5. Drain the pasta mixture and return to the pan
6. Stir in soured cream
7. Garnish with parsley and serve

TOFU SALAD

Serves: **1**

Prep Time: **5** Minutes

Cook Time: **5** Minutes

Total Time: **10** Minutes

INGREDIENTS

- 1 pack tofu
- 1 cup chopped vegetables (carrots, cucumber)

DRESSING

- 1 tablespoon sesame oil
- 1 tablespoon mustard
- 1 tablespoon brown rice vinegar
- 1 tablespoon soya sauce

DIRECTIONS

1. In a bowl combine all ingredients together and mix well
2. Add salad dressing, toss well and serve

COUSCOUS SALAD

Serves: *1*
Prep Time: 5   Minutes

Cook Time: 5   Minutes

Total Time: *10*   Minutes

INGREDIENTS

- 1 cup cooked couscous
- ¼ cup pine nuts
- 1 shallot
- 2 cloves garlic
- 1 can chickpeas
- 2 oz. low fat cheese
- 1 zucchini

DIRECTIONS

1. In a bowl combine all ingredients together and mix well
2. Add salad dressing, toss well and serve

BROCCOLI SALAD

Serves: *1*

Prep Time: 5   Minutes

Cook Time: 5   Minutes

Total Time: *10*   Minutes

INGREDIENTS

- 1 broccoli
- 1 cup tomatoes
- 1 cup feta cheese
- ½ cup almonds
- 1 cup lemon salad dressing

DIRECTIONS

1. In a bowl combine all ingredients together and mix well
2. Add salad dressing, toss well and serve

Serves: *1*

Prep Time: *5*   Minutes

Cook Time: *5*   Minutes

Total Time: *10*   Minutes

INGREDIENTS

- ½ cup sun-dried tomatoes
- ½ cup parmesan
- 1 tablespoon lemon juice
- 1 garlic clove
- ¼ cup olive oil
- 1 cup lemon salad dressing

DIRECTIONS

1. In a bowl combine all ingredients together and mix well
2. Add salad dressing, toss well and serve

CARROT-EDAMAME SALAD

Serves: 1
Prep Time: 5   Minutes
Cook Time: 5   Minutes
Total Time: 10   Minutes

INGREDIENTS

- 4 oz. romaine lettuce
- 1 cup edamame
- 1 cup cabbage
- ¼ cup red onion
- 1 red bell pepper
- ¼ cup cilantro

DIRECTIONS

1. In a bowl combine all ingredients together and mix well
2. Add salad dressing, toss well and serve

CAULIFLOWER & FARRO SALAD

Serves: *1*
Prep Time: *5*   Minutes

Cook Time: *5*   Minutes

Total Time: *10*   Minutes

INGREDIENTS

- 1 cauliflower
- 1 tablespoon olive oil
- ¼ tsp black pepper
- 1 cup cooked Farro
- 2 garlic cloves
- ¼ cup feta cheese
- 1 avocado

DIRECTIONS

1. In a bowl combine all ingredients together and mix well
2. Add salad dressing, toss well and serve

ARUGULA &CHICKPEA SALAD

Serves: *1*

Prep Time: *5*   Minutes

Cook Time: *5*   Minutes

Total Time: *10*   Minutes

INGREDIENTS

- 1 cup cooked chickpeas
- 2 carrots
- ¼ cup feta cheese
- 4 cups arugula
- 1 cup lemon salad dressing

DIRECTIONS

1. In a bowl combine all ingredients together and mix well
2. Add salad dressing, toss well and serve

CHEESE MACARONI

Serves: *1*

Prep Time: *10*   Minutes

Cook Time: *20*   Minutes

Total Time: *30*   Minutes

INGREDIENTS

- 1 lb. macaroni
- 1 cup cheddar cheese
- 1 cup Monterey Jack cheese
- 1 cup mozzarella cheese
- ¼ tsp salt
- ¼ tsp pepper

DIRECTIONS

1. In a pot bring water to a boil
2. Add pasta and cook until al dente
3. In a bowl combine all cheese together and add it to the pasta
4. When ready transfer to a bowl, add salt, pepper and serve

POTATO CASSEROLE

Serves: 2

Prep Time: *10*   Minutes

Cook Time: *20*   Minutes

Total Time: *30*   Minutes

INGREDIENTS

- 5-6 large potatoes
- ¼ cup sour cream
- ½ cup butter
- 5-6 bacon strips
- 1-2 cups mozzarella cheese
- ¼ cup heavy cream

DIRECTIONS

1. Place the potatoes in a pot with boiling water, cook until tender
2. Place the potatoes in a bowl, add sour cream, butter, cheese and mix well
3. In a baking dish place the bacon strips and cover with potato mixture
4. Add remaining mozzarella cheese on top
5. Bake at 325 F for 15-18 minutes or until the mozzarella is fully melted
6. When ready remove from the oven and serve

CHEESE STUFFED SHELLS

Serves: 2

Prep Time: **10** Minutes

Cook Time: **30** Minutes

Total Time: **40** Minutes

INGREDIENTS

- 2-3 cups macaroni
- 2 cups cream cheese
- 1 cup spaghetti sauce
- 1 cup onions
- 1 cup mozzarella cheese

DIRECTIONS

1. In a pot boil water and add shells
2. Cook for 12-15 minutes
3. In a baking dish add spaghetti sauce
4. In a bowl combine cream cheese, onion and set aside
5. Add cream cheese to the shells and place them into the baking dish
6. Bake at 325 F for 30 minutes or until golden brown
7. When ready remove from the oven and serve

POTATO SOUP

Serves: **4-6**
Prep Time: **10** Minutes
Cook Time: **50** Minutes
Total Time: **60** Minutes

INGREDIENTS

- 1 onion
- 2-3 carrots
- 2 tablespoons flour
- 5-6 large potatoes
- 2 cups milk
- 2 cups bouillon
- 1 cup water
- 2 cups milk
- 1 tsp salt
- 1 tsp pepper

DIRECTIONS

1. In a saucepan melt butter and sauce carrots, garlic and onion for 4-5 minutes
2. Add flour, milk, potatoes, bouillon and cook for another 15-20 minutes

3. Add pepper and remaining ingredients and cook on low heat for 20-30 minutes

4. When ready remove from heat and serve

CHICKEN ALFREDO

Serves: 2

Prep Time: **10**   Minutes

Cook Time: **20**   Minutes

Total Time: **30**   Minutes

INGREDIENTS

- 2-3 chicken breasts
- 1 lb. rotini
- 1 cup parmesan cheese
- 1 cup olive oil
- 1 tsp salt
- 1 tsp black pepper
- 1 tsp parsley

DIRECTIONS

1. In a pot add the rotini and cook on low heat for 12-15 minutes
2. In a frying pan heat olive oil, add chicken, salt, parsley, and cook until the chicken is brown
3. Drain the rotini and place the rotini in pan with chicken
4. Cook for 2-3 minutes
5. When ready remove from heat and serve with parmesan cheese on top

BUTTERNUT SQUASH PIZZA

Serves: **4-6**
Prep Time: **10** Minutes

Cook Time: **15** Minutes

Total Time: **25** Minutes

INGREDIENTS

- 2 cups butternut squash
- ¼ tsp salt
- 1 pizza crust
- 5-6 tablespoons alfredo sauce
- 1 tsp olive oil
- 4-5 cups baby spinach
- 2-3 oz. goat cheese

DIRECTIONS

1. Place the pizza crust on a baking dish and spread the alfredo sauce
2. In a skillet sauté spinach and place it over the pizza crust
3. Add goat cheese, butternut squash, olive oil and salt
4. Bake pizza at 425 F for 8-10 minutes
5. When ready remove from the oven and serve

PENNE WITH ASPARAGUS

Serves: **2**

Prep Time: **10** Minutes

Cook Time: **20** Minutes

Total Time: **30** Minutes

INGREDIENTS

- 6-7 oz. penne pasta
- 2-3 bacon slices
- ¼ cup red onion
- 2 cups asparagus
- 1 cup chicken broth
- 2-3 cups spinach leaves
- ¼ cup parmesan cheese

DIRECTIONS

1. Cook pasta until al dente
2. In a skillet cook bacon until crispy and set aside
3. In a pan add onion, asparagus, broth and cook on low heat for 5-10 minutes
4. Add spinach, cheese, pepper, pasta and cook for another 5-6 minutes
5. When ready sprinkle bacon and serve

NOODLE SOUP

Serves: **4**

Prep Time: **10** Minutes

Cook Time: **20** Minutes

Total Time: **30** Minutes

INGREDIENTS

- 2-3 cups water
- 1 can chicken broth
- 1 tablespoon olive oil
- ¼ red onion
- ¼ cup celery
- ¼ tsp salt
- ¼ tsp black pepper
- 5-6 oz. fusilli pasta
- 2 cups chicken breast
- 2 tablespoons parsley

DIRECTIONS

1. In a pot boil water with broth
2. In a saucepan heat oil, add carrot, pepper, celery, onion, salt and sauté until tender
3. Add broth mixture to the mixture and pasta

4. Cook until al dente and stir in chicken breast, cook until chicken breast is tender

5. When ready remove from heat, stir in parsley and serve

TOMATO WRAP

Serves: **4**

Prep Time: **5**   Minutes

Cook Time: **15**   Minutes

Total Time: **20**   Minutes

INGREDIENTS

- 1 cup corn
- 1 cup tomatoes
- 1 cup pickles
- 1 tablespoon olive oil
- 1 tablespoon mayonnaise
- 6-7 turkey slices
- 2-3 whole-wheat tortillas
- 1 cup romaine lettuce

DIRECTIONS

1. In a bowl combine tomatoes, pickles, olive oil, corn and set aside
2. Place the turkey slices over the tortillas and top with tomato mixture and mayonnaise
3. Roll and serve

THYME COD

Serves: **2**

Prep Time: **5**   Minutes

Cook Time: **15** Minutes

Total Time: **20** Minutes

INGREDIENTS

- 1 tablespoon olive oil
- ½ red onion
- 1 can tomatoes
- 2-3 springs thyme
- 2-3 cod fillets

DIRECTIONS

1. In a frying pan heat olive oil and sauté onion, stir in tomatoes, spring thyme and cook for 5-6 minutes
2. Add cod fillets, cover and cook for 5-6 minutes per side
3. When ready remove from heat and serve

Serves: 2
Prep Time: **10**   Minutes
Cook Time: **20**   Minutes
Total Time: **30**   Minutes

INGREDIENTS

- 1 tablespoon cornstarch
- 1 garlic clove
- ¼ cup olive oil
- ¼ head broccoli
- ¼ cup show peas
- ½ cup carrots
- ¼ cup green beans
- 1 tablespoon soy sauce
- ½ cup onion

DIRECTIONS

1. In a bowl combine garlic, olive oil, cornstarch and mix well
2. Add the rest of the ingredients and toss to coat
3. In a skillet cook vegetables mixture until tender
4. When ready transfer to a plate garnish with ginger and serve

GINGER COLADA SMOOTHIE

Serves: *1*

Prep Time: 5   Minutes

Cook Time: 5   Minutes

Total Time: *10*   Minutes

INGREDIENTS

- 1 tablespoon ginger
- ½ cup lemon juice
- 1 cup pineapple
- 1 banana
- 1 handful spinach
- 1 handful kale
- 1 cup ice

DIRECTIONS

1. In a blender place all ingredients and blend until smooth
2. Pour smoothie in a glass and serve

RAINBOW SMOOTHIE

Serves: **1**

Prep Time: **5** Minutes

Cook Time: **5** Minutes

Total Time: **10** Minutes

INGREDIENTS

- ¼ cup grapefruit
- ¼ cup watermelon
- 1 cup raspberries
- 1 cup pomegranate
- 1 cup ice

DIRECTIONS

1. In a blender place all ingredients and blend until smooth
2. Pour smoothie in a glass and serve

ACAI SMOOTHIE

Serves: **1**
Prep Time: **5**   Minutes
Cook Time: **5**   Minutes
Total Time: **10**   Minutes

INGREDIENTS

- 1 cup acai puree
- 1 banana
- 1 cup pomegranate juice
- 1 kiwi
- ½ lemon

DIRECTIONS

1. In a blender place all ingredients and blend until smooth
2. Pour smoothie in a glass and serve

BERRY SMOOTHIE

Serves:	*1*	
Prep Time:	*5*	Minutes
Cook Time:	*5*	Minutes
Total Time:	*10*	Minutes

INGREDIENTS

- 1 cup strawberries
- 1 cup blueberries
- ½ cup orange juice
- ½ cup coconut water
- 1 cup ice

DIRECTIONS

1. In a blender place all ingredients and blend until smooth
2. Pour smoothie in a glass and serve

GREEN SMOOTHIE

Serves: *1*
Prep Time: 5   Minutes

Cook Time: 5   Minutes

Total Time: *10*   Minutes

INGREDIENTS

- 2 stalks celery
- 4 cups spinach
- 1 pear
- 1 banana
- 1 tablespoon lime juice
- 1 cup coconut water
- 1 cup ice

DIRECTIONS

1. In a blender place all ingredients and blend until smooth
2. Pour smoothie in a glass and serve

Serves: *1*

Prep Time: 5   Minutes

Cook Time: 5   Minutes

Total Time: *10* Minutes

INGREDIENTS

- 2 cups kiwi
- 2 bananas
- 2 mangoes
- ½ cup pineapple
- 1 cup ice
- 1 cup coconut water
- 1 tablespoon honey

DIRECTIONS

1. In a blender place all ingredients and blend until smooth
2. Pour smoothie in a glass and serve

SOY SMOOTHIE

Serves: **1**

Prep Time: **5** Minutes

Cook Time: **5** Minutes

Total Time: **10** Minutes

INGREDIENTS

- 2 cups blueberries
- 1 cup soy vanilla yogurt
- 1 cup soy milk
- 1 tsp vanilla essence

DIRECTIONS

1. In a blender place all ingredients and blend until smooth
2. Pour smoothie in a glass and serve

POWER SMOOTHIE

Serves: **1**

Prep Time: **5** Minutes

Cook Time: **5** Minutes

Total Time: **10** Minutes

INGREDIENTS

- 1 cup kale
- ¼ cup greens
- ¼ cup baby spinach
- ¼ cup greens
- ½ cup pineapple
- ½ cup blueberries
- 1 cup almon milk

DIRECTIONS

1. In a blender place all ingredients and blend until smooth
2. Pour smoothie in a glass and serve

OAT SMOOTHIE

Serves: **1**

Prep Time: 5   Minutes

Cook Time: 5   Minutes

Total Time: **10**   Minutes

INGREDIENTS

- 1 cup orange juice
- ¼ cup oats
- 1 tablespoon flaxseed meal
- 1 tablespoon honey
- 1 banana
- 1 cup ice

DIRECTIONS

1. In a blender place all ingredients and blend until smooth
2. Pour smoothie in a glass and serve

APPLE SMOOTHIE

Serves: *1*

Prep Time: 5   Minutes

Cook Time: 5   Minutes

Total Time: **10**   Minutes

INGREDIENTS

- 2 green apples
- 1 banana
- ½ cup almond milk
- 1 cup ice
- ¼ cup vanilla yogurt
- 1 tsp cinnamon
- ¼ tsp nutmeg

DIRECTIONS

1. In a blender place all ingredients and blend until smooth
2. Pour smoothie in a glass and serve

SECOND COOKBOOK

MUSHROOM OMELETTE

Serves: *1*
Prep Time: 5   Minutes

Cook Time: *10*   Minutes

Total Time: *15*   Minutes

INGREDIENTS

- 2 eggs
- ¼ tsp salt
- ¼ tsp black pepper
- 1 tablespoon olive oil
- ¼ cup cheese
- ¼ tsp basil
- 1 cup mushrooms

DIRECTIONS

1. In a bowl combine all ingredients together and mix well
2. In a skillet heat olive oil and pour the egg mixture
3. Cook for 1-2 minutes per side
4. When ready remove omelette from the skillet and serve

Serves: **4**

Prep Time: **10**   Minutes

Cook Time: **30**   Minutes

Total Time: **40**   Minutes

INGREDIENTS

- ¼ lb. cheddar cheese
- 2 jalapeno peppers
- ½ lb. almond flour
- 1 tsp baking powder
- ½ tsp baking soda
- ¼ tsp salt
- ¼ tsp paprika powder
- ¼ tsp thyme
- ¼ cayenne powder
- 1 egg
- 1 tablespoon apple cider vinegar
- 5 tablespoons butter
- 4 tablespoons almond milk
- 4 tablespoons sour cream

DIRECTIONS

1. Preheat the oven to 325 F
2. In a bowl add all wet ingredients and mix well
3. In another bowl add all dry ingredients and pour over the wet ingredients and mix well
4. Spoon mixture into a silicone tart mold
5. Bake for 20-25 minutes, remove and serve

MORNING CARROT CAKE

Serves: **12**
Prep Time: **10**   Minutes

Cook Time: **35**   Minutes

Total Time: **45**   Minutes

INGREDIENTS

- 1 recipe cream cheese
- 1 recipe dairy free whipped frosting
- ½ lb. carrot
- 3 eggs
- 2 oz. coconut oil
- 4 oz. almond milk
- ½ lb. almond flour
- 1 oz. coconut flour
- 1 tsp stevia powder
- ½ cup erythritol
- 1 tsp cinnamon
- ½ tsp ground cloves
- ½ tsp cardamom powder
- ½ tsp allspice
- ½ tsp baking soda

DIRECTIONS

1. Preheat the oven to 325 F
2. In a bowl add all wet ingredients and mix well
3. In another bowl add all dry ingredients and pour over the wet ingredients and mix well
4. Pour the carrot cake batter inside your casserole dish
5. Bake for 30-35 minutes, remove and serve

LOW CARB OATMEAL

Serves: 2

Prep Time: 5   Minutes

Cook Time: 30   Minutes

Total Time: 35   Minutes

INGREDIENTS

- 2 oz. walnuts
- 2 oz. pecans
- 1 oz. sunflower seeds
- 0,7 L unsweetened almond milk
- 3 tablespoons chia seeds
- ¼ tsp stevia powder
- ½ tsp cinnamon

DIRECTIONS

1. In a blender add walnuts, sunflower seeds, pecans and blend until smooth
2. In a pot add the rest of ingredients and blender mixture, simmer for 25-30 minutes on low heat
3. When ready, remove and serve

DAIRY-FREE BREAD

Serves: **6**
Prep Time: **10** Minutes

Cook Time: **20** Minutes

Total Time: **30** Minutes

INGREDIENTS

- 3 egg whites
- 3 egg yolks
- 3 tablespoons mayonnaise
- ½ tsp cream of tartar
- ½ tsp garlic powder
- ¼ tsp parsley

DIRECTIONS

1. Preheat oven to 375 F
2. In a bowl mix cream of tartar and egg whites
3. In another bow mix the rest of the ingredients with a hand mixer
4. Fold the firm meringue into the yolk mixture
5. On a baking sheet add ¼ cup of the foam and spread the mixture
6. Bake for 15-20 minutes
7. Remove and serve

Serves: *1*

Prep Time: *5*   Minutes

Cook Time: *5*   Minutes

Total Time: *10*   Minutes

INGREDIENTS

- 2 tablespoons pumpkin puree
- 2 tablespoons almond utter
- 1 tsp unsalted butter
- 1 egg
- ¼ tsp stevia powder
- ½ tsp baking powder
- ½ tsp cinnamon
- ¼ tsp ground cloves
- ¼ tsp nutmeg
- ¼ tsp ground cardamon

DIRECTIONS

1. In a mug add all ingredients and mix well
2. Microwave for 2-3 minutes
3. Remove, add melted chocolate and serve

CHEESY BISCUITS

Serves: **6**

Prep Time: **10** Minutes

Cook Time: **30** Minutes

Total Time: **40** Minutes

INGREDIENTS

- ¼ lb. shredded gouda
- olive oil spray
- 1 cup almond flour
- 1 tsp baking powder
- ½ tsp baking soda
- ¼ tsp salt
- 1 tsp parsley
- ¼ tsp garlic powder
- 1 tsp rosemary
- ¼ tsp onion powder
- ¼ tsp sour cream
- 1 tablespoon butter
- 1 tablespoon apple cider vinegar
- 2 eggs
- 1 oz. almond milk

DIRECTIONS

1. Preheat oven to 350 F
2. In a bowl add all wet ingredients and mix well
3. In another bowl add all dry ingredients and pour over the wet ingredients and mix well
4. Spoon the mixture into a silicone tart mold
5. Bake for 20-25 minutes
6. Remove and serve

EGG AND VEGGIES BREAKFAST

Serves: **2**
Prep Time: **5**   Minutes

Cook Time: **5**   Minutes

Total Time: **10**   Minutes

INGREDIENTS

- 2 eggs
- 1 tablespoon water
- 1 tablespoon baby spinach
- 1 tablespoon mushrooms
- cherry tomatoes

DIRECTIONS

1. Coat 8 oz. ramekin with cooking spray
2. Add all the ingredients and mix well
3. Microwave for 1-2 minutes
4. Top with tomatoes and serve

SUMMER EGGS

Serves: **1**

Prep Time: **5** Minutes

Cook Time: **10** Minutes

Total Time: **15** Minutes

INGREDIENTS

- 1 tablespoon olive oil
- 1 zucchini
- 6 oz. pack tomatoes
- 1 garlic clove
- 3 eggs
- 4-5 basil leaves

DIRECTIONS

1. In a frying pan add zucchini, fry for 3-4 minutes
2. Add garlic, tomatoes cook for 2-3 minutes and add seasoning
3. Crack in the eggs and cover the pan, cook for 2-3 minutes
4. Top with basil leaves and serve

ALMOND BUTTER CEREAL

Serves: **4**

Prep Time: **10**   Minutes

Cook Time: **30**   Minutes

Total Time: **40**   Minutes

INGREDIENTS

- ½ cup flax seed meal
- ½ cup water
- 1 tablespoon almond butter
- ½ tsp cinnamon
- ¼ raisins

DIRECTIONS

1. Pour boiling water over flax seed meal, stir in cinnamon, almond butter and let it stand for 2-3 minutes
2. Serve with raisins

OVERNIGHT OATS

Serves: **2**

Prep Time: **5**   Minutes

Cook Time: **5**   Minutes

Total Time: **10**   Minutes

INGREDIENTS

- 1 cup Greek yogurt
- ½ cup uncooked oats
- ½ apple
- 8 grapes
- 5 walnuts
- 1 tablespoon almond milk
- 2 drops liquid stevia
- cinnamon

DIRECTIONS

1. In a bowl add all ingredients together and mix well
2. Store in a glass and refrigerate
3. Serve in the morning

AVOCADO TOAST

Serves: **1**
Prep Time: **5**   Minutes

Cook Time: **5**   Minutes

Total Time: **10**   Minutes

INGREDIENTS

- Premade guacamole
- 2 eggs
- 2 slices tomato
- 2 slices gluten-free bread

DIRECTIONS

1. Spread the guacamole over your bread
2. Top with scrambled eggs, salt and tomato slices
3. Serve when ready

BREAKFAST SAUSAGE WITH SWEET POTATO

Serves: *3*
Prep Time: *10*   Minutes
Cook Time: *50*   Minutes
Total Time: *60*   Minutes

INGREDIENTS

- 1 sweet potato
- ½ tablespoon coconut butter
- 3 Applegate naturals chicken
- Apple breakfast sausage

DIRECTIONS

1. Bake sweet potato at 375 F for 45-50 minutes
2. Cook the sausage according to the indications
3. Top the sweet potato with coconut butter and serve

GREEN PEA PARATHAS

Serves: **4**

Prep Time: **10**   Minutes

Cook Time: **30**   Minutes

Total Time: **40**   Minutes

INGREDIENTS

- ½ CUP whole wheat flour
- ¼ cup boiled green peas
- 1 tsp green chilies
- 1 tablespoon low fat curds
- salt

DIRECTIONS

1. In a blender add green peas and blend until smooth
2. Mix all ingredients with the green peas mixture into a soft dough
3. Divide into 4-6 servings
4. Cook each Paratha in a pan until golden brown
5. Remove and serve

SPORUTS MISAL

Serves: **4**

Prep Time: **10** Minutes

Cook Time: **30** Minutes

Total Time: **40** Minutes

INGREDIENTS

- 2 cups mixed sprouts
- 1 tsp cumin seeds
- 1 tsp chili paste
- ½ tsp cloves powder
- ½ tsp cinnamon powder
- 1 tsp oil
- 1 pinch of salt

DIRECTIONS

1. In a frying pan add cumin seeds, chili paste and cook for 1-2 minutes
2. Add the rest of ingredients and cook for 2-3 minutes
3. Serve the sprouts mixture with onions or tomatoes

KARELA THEPLA

Serves: **4**

Prep Time: **10** Minutes

Cook Time: **30** Minutes

Total Time: **40** Minutes

INGREDIENTS

- ½ cup bitter gourd
- 1 cup whole wheat flour
- ½ cup bajra
- ¼ tsp chopped garlic
- ¼ tsp turmeric powder
- 1 tsp chili powder
- 1 tsp coriander
- 1 tsp oil
- salt

DIRECTIONS

1. In a bowl mix all ingredients
2. Divide dough into 8-10 portions
3. Heat a non-stick griddle and cook until golden brown
4. Remove and serve

Serves: *1*
Prep Time: 5   Minutes

Cook Time: 5   Minutes

Total Time: *10*   Minutes

INGREDIENTS

- 1 cup Greek yogurt
- ¼ cup oats
- 1 tablespoon almond milk
- 1 tsp chia seeds
- 1 tablespoon honey
- ¼ cup blueberries
- ¼ cup apples

DIRECTIONS

1. In a bowl combine all ingredients together
2. Add honey and mix well
3. Serve when ready

PANCAKES

BANANA PANCAKES

Serves: **4**

Prep Time: **10** Minutes

Cook Time: **20** Minutes

Total Time: **30** Minutes

INGREDIENTS

- 1 cup whole wheat flour
- ¼ tsp baking soda
- ¼ tsp baking powder
- 1 cup mashed banana
- 2 eggs
- 1 cup milk

DIRECTIONS

1. In a bowl combine all ingredients together and mix well
2. In a skillet heat olive oil
3. Pour ¼ of the batter and cook each pancake for 1-2 minutes per side
4. When ready remove from heat and serve

SPROUTS PANCAKES

Serves: **4**

Prep Time: 5   Minutes

Cook Time: 5   Minutes

Total Time: **10**   Minutes

INGREDIENTS

- 1 cup sprouts
- 1 tablespoon carrot
- ½ cup spinach
- ½ cup fenugreek
- 1 tablespoon besan
- ½ tsp turmeric powder
- ½ tsp cumin seeds
- 1 tsp green chili paste
- 2 tsp soil
- salt

DIRECTIONS

1. In a blender mix sprouts with water and blend until smooth
2. Transfer to a bowl and add he rest of ingredients and mix well
3. Pour mixture into a frying pan and cook for 1-2 minutes per side
4. Repeat with the remaining batter and serve when ready

ZUCCHINI PANCAKE

Serves: 2
Prep Time: 5   Minutes
Cook Time: 5   Minutes
Total Time: **10** Minutes

INGREDIENTS

- ¾ cup zucchini
- ½ cup carrot
- ½ cup rice flour
- ½ cup besan
- 1 tablespoon coriander
- 1 tsp green chilies
- 2 tsp oil
- salt

DIRECTIONS

1. In a bowl mix all ingredients and add ¼ cup water
2. Pour batter into a frying pan and cook for 1-2 minutes per side
3. Repeat with the remaining batter and serve when ready

CHEESE PANCAKES

Serves: **4**

Prep Time: **10** Minutes

Cook Time: **10** Minutes

Total Time: **20** Minutes

INGREDIENTS

- 1 cup almond flour
- ¼ tsp baking soda
- 1 tablespoon brown sugar
- salt
- 3 eggs
- 1 cup cottage cheese
- ¼ cup milk
- 1 tablespoon olive oil

DIRECTIONS

1. In a bowl combine all ingredients together
2. Heat oil in a skillet and pour mixture pancakes
3. Cook each pancake for 1-2 minutes per side
4. When ready remove from the skillet and serve

SIMPLE PANCAKES

Serves: 2
Prep Time: 5   Minutes
Cook Time: 5   Minutes
Total Time: 10   Minutes

INGREDIENTS

- 1 banana
- 2 eggs
- 1 cup milk

DIRECTIONS

1. In a bowl combine all ingredients together
2. Pour mixture into a skillet
3. Cook for 1-2 minutes per side
4. When ready remove to a plate and serve

PEANUT BUTTER SMOOTHIE

Serves: 2

Prep Time: 5   Minutes

Cook Time: 5   Minutes

Total Time: *10*   Minutes

INGREDIENTS

- 1 cup milk
- 1 large banana
- 3 tablespoons peanut butter

DIRECTIONS

1. In a blender place all ingredients and blend until smooth
2. Pour smoothie in a glass and serve

BLUEBERRY & SPINACH SMOOTHIE

Serves: 2
Prep Time: 5   Minutes

Cook Time: 5   Minutes

Total Time: 10 Minutes

INGREDIENTS

- 2 cups spinach leaves
- 1 banana
- 1 cup blueberries
- 1 cup milk

DIRECTIONS

1. In a blender place all ingredients and blend until smooth
2. Pour smoothie in a glass and serve

Serves: *1*
Prep Time: *5*   Minutes
Cook Time: *5*   Minutes
Total Time: *10* Minutes

INGREDIENTS

- ¼ orange juice
- 1 cup yogurt
- 1 banana
- 4 strawberries

DIRECTIONS

1. In a blender place all ingredients and blend until smooth
2. Pour smoothie in a glass and serve

CREAMY BANANA SMOOTHIE

Serves: *1*
Prep Time: *5*   Minutes

Cook Time: *5*   Minutes

Total Time: *10*   Minutes

INGREDIENTS

- 1 cup milk
- ½ cup yogurt
- 1 banana

DIRECTIONS

1. In a blender place all ingredients and blend until smooth
2. Pour smoothie in a glass and serve

Serves: **2**

Prep Time: **5**   Minutes

Cook Time: **5**   Minutes

Total Time: **10** Minutes

INGREDIENTS

- 1 cup milk
- ½ avocado
- 1 banana

DIRECTIONS

1. In a blender place all ingredients and blend until smooth
2. Pour smoothie in a glass and serve

Serves: **1**

Prep Time: **5** Minutes

Cook Time: **5** Minutes

Total Time: **10** Minutes

INGREDIENTS

- 1 cup water
- 3 cubes ice
- ½ cucumber
- 2 cups spinach
- 2 cups pineapple

DIRECTIONS

1. In a blender place all ingredients and blend until smooth
2. Pour smoothie in a glass and serve

Serves: *1*
Prep Time: 5   Minutes

Cook Time: 5   Minutes

Total Time: *10* Minutes

INGREDIENTS

- 1 avocado
- 2 kiwis
- ½ cup broccoli
- 1 cup orange juice

DIRECTIONS

1. In a blender place all ingredients and blend until smooth
2. Pour smoothie in a glass and serve

MANGO SMOOTHIE

Serves: *1*

Prep Time: 5   Minutes

Cook Time: 5   Minutes

Total Time: *10*   Minutes

INGREDIENTS

- 1 cup milk
- 1 cup yogurt
- 1 banana
- 1 cup mango
- 1 teaspoon vanilla extract

DIRECTIONS

1. In a blender place all ingredients and blend until smooth
2. Pour smoothie in a glass and serve

COOKIES

BREAKFAST COOKIES

Serves: **8-12**

Prep Time: **5**   Minutes

Cook Time: **15**   Minutes

Total Time: **20**   Minutes

INGREDIENTS

- 1 cup rolled oats
- ¼ cup applesauce
- ½ tsp vanilla extract
- 3 tablespoons chocolate chips
- 2 tablespoons dried fruits
- 1 tsp cinnamon

DIRECTIONS

1. Preheat the oven to 325 F
2. In a bowl combine all ingredients together and mix well
3. Scoop cookies using an ice cream scoop
4. Place cookies onto a prepared baking sheet
5. Place in the oven for 12-15 minutes or until the cookies are done
6. When ready remove from the oven and serve

LOW CARB MORNING COOKIES

Serves: **36**

Prep Time: **15** Minutes

Cook Time: **15** Minutes

Total Time: **30** Minutes

INGREDIENTS

- ½ almond butter
- 1 cup almond flour
- ¼ oat fiber
- ½ tsp salt
- 5 tablespoons powdered erythritol
- ½ tsp stevia powder
- 5 tablespoons chocolate chips
- 1 tablespoon coconut oil

DIRECTIONS

1. Preheat the oven to 325 F
2. In a bowl add almond flour, erythritol, stevia, salt, butter, oat fiber and mix with a stand mixer for a couple of minutes
3. Place the dough on top of a parchment paper and into small pieces using biscuit cutters
4. Bake for 10-15 minutes or until golden brown
5. Remove and dip into chocolate, let it solidify and serve

PUMPKIN CHOCOLATE CHIP COOKIES

Serves: *10*

Prep Time: *10*   Minutes

Cook Time: *30*   Minutes

Total Time: *40*   Minutes

INGREDIENTS

- ½ cup almond butter
- ½ cup pumpkin puree
- ½ cup erythritol
- ½ tsp ginger powder
- ½ tsp nutmeg
- ½ tsp cardamom powder
- ½ tsp cloves
- 1 tsp cinnamon

DIRECTIONS

1. Preheat the oven to 325 F
2. In a bowl mix all ingredients using a hand mixer
3. Place parchment paper oven a baking tray and scoop batter over the baking trays
4. Bake for 20-25 minutes, remove and serve

Serves: **20**

Prep Time: **10**   Minutes

Cook Time: **20**   Minutes

Total Time: **30**   Minutes

INGREDIENTS

- 1 lb. hazelnuts
- 1 tablespoon coconut oil
- 3 tablespoons cocoa powder
- 4 tablespoons powdered erythritol

DIRECTIONS

1. Place the hazelnuts on an oven tray and bake at 300 F for 15-18 minutes
2. Place the hazelnuts in a blender and blend until smooth
3. Add coconut oil and blend for another 10-12 minutes, longer is better
4. Add erythritol, cocoa powder and blend for another 4-5 minutes
5. Remove and serve

BANANA BARS

Serves: **4**

Prep Time: **10** Minutes

Cook Time: **30** Minutes

Total Time: **40** Minutes

INGREDIENTS

- 2 bananas
- 1 tablespoon honey
- 2 tablespoons coconut flour
- 1 cup almond flour
- ½ cup peanut butter
- ½ cup olive oil
- 3 eggs
- ½ tsp salt
- ¼ cup walnuts
- ½ cup raisins
- ½ tsp baking soda

CARAMELIZED TOPPING

- 5 medjool dates
- 1 tablespoon butter
- ½ cup water
- dash salt
- 1 tsp vanilla extract

DIRECTIONS

1. Preheat oven to 325 F
2. In a bowl mix peanut butter, honey, coconut oil, eggs and mix
3. Add coconut flour, salt, baking soda, almond flour and beat well
4. Stir in raisins and walnuts
5. Line a baking dish and spread batter in baking dish
6. Bake for 20 minutes, remove from oven and let it cool
7. In a saucepan add topping ingredients and cook for 12-15 minutes
8. Remove from heat and spread topping over bars

MUFFINS

BREAKFAST MUFFINS

Serves: **8-12**

Prep Time: **10** Minutes

Cook Time: **20** Minutes

Total Time: **30** Minutes

INGREDIENTS

- 8 eggs
- ¼ tsp salt
- 2 onions
- 1 cup ham
- ¼ tsp garlic powder
- ¼ cup mushrooms
- 1 cup cheddar cheese
- ¼ cup spinach

DIRECTIONS

1. In a bowl combine we ingredients and dry ingredients together
2. Fold in mushrooms and mix well
3. Pour mixture into 8-12 prepared muffin cups
4. Bake at 375 for 18-20 minutes
5. When ready remove from the oven and serve

Serves: **8-12**
Prep Time: **10**   Minutes

Cook Time: **25**   Minutes

Total Time: **35**   Minutes

INGREDIENTS

- 2 cups almond flour
- 1 cup brown sugar
- 1 tablespoon pumpkin spice
- 1 tsp baking soda
- 2 eggs
- 1 cup pumpkin puree
- ¼ cup olive oil

DIRECTIONS

1. In a bowl combine dry ingredients and wet ingredients together
2. Add pumpkin puree and mix well
3. Pour mixture into 8-12 muffin cups
4. Cook for 20-25 minutes at 375 F
5. When ready remove from the oven and serve

STRAWBERRY MUFFINS

Serves: **8-12**

Prep Time: **10**   Minutes

Cook Time: **25**   Minutes

Total Time: **35**   Minutes

INGREDIENTS

- ¼ cup olive oil
- ½ cup brown sugar
- 1 egg
- 2 cups almond flour
- 1 tsp baking soda
- ¼ cup almond milk
- ¼ tsp vanilla extract
- 1 cup strawberries

DIRECTIONS

1. In a bowl combine dry ingredients and wet ingredients together
2. Add strawberries and mix well
3. Pour mixture into 8-12 prepared muffin cups
4. Cook for 20-25 minutes at 375 F
5. When ready remove from the oven and serve

ZUCCHINI MUFFINS

Serves: **8-12**
Prep Time: **10**   Minutes

Cook Time: **20**   Minutes

Total Time: **30**   Minutes

INGREDIENTS

- 2 eggs
- 1 cup sugar
- 1 tsp vanilla extract
- 2 cups zucchini
- 2 cups almond flour
- ¼ tsp salt
- ¼ tsp cinnamon
- 1 tsp baking soda
- ¼ tsp baking powder

DIRECTIONS

1. Preheat the oven to 350 F
2. In a bowl combine dry ingredients and wet ingredients together
3. Pour mixture into 8-12 prepare muffin cups and fill 2/3 of the cup
4. Bake for 12-15 minutes
5. When ready remove muffins from the oven and serve

PUMPKIN MUFFINS

Serves: 6
Prep Time: 5   Minutes

Cook Time: 20   Minutes

Total Time: 25   Minutes

INGREDIENTS

- 1/3 lb. pumpkin puree
- 1/3 lb. almond butter
- 2 tablespoons coconut oil
- ¾ tsp stevia powder
- ¼ tsp cinnamon
- ½ tsp ground cloves
- ½ tsp cardamom powder
- ½ tsp ginger
- 1 tsp baking powder
- ½ tsp baking soda
- 3 eggs

DIRECTIONS

1. Preheat the oven to 350 F
2. In a bowl mix all ingredients and pour batter into 6 muffin cups
3. Bake for 15-20 minutes, remove and serve

THIRD COOKBOOK

BANANA AND APPLE PANCAKES

Serves: *3*
Prep Time: *5*   Minutes

Cook Time: *5*   Minutes

Total Time: *10*   Minutes

INGREDIENTS

- 1 apple
- 5 eggs
- 2 bananas
- 1 tablespoon coconut oil

DIRECTIONS

1. In a bowl mash the bananas and apples
2. Crack the eggs and mix them all together
3. In a frying pan pour one-two spoons of mixture
4. Cook each pancake for 1-2 minutes per side
5. Remove and serve with honey

YOGURT WITH MIXED BERRIES

Serves: *1*
Prep Time: *5*   Minutes

Cook Time: *5*   Minutes

Total Time: *10*   Minutes

INGREDIENTS

- 3 cups yogurt
- ½ cup almonds
- ¼ cup blueberries
- 1 cup strawberries
- ½ tsp lemon juice

DIRECTIONS

1. In a bowl place all ingredients
2. Mixed well and refrigerate overnight
3. Serve in the morning

Serves: *1*
Prep Time: *5*   Minutes

Cook Time: *5*   Minutes

Total Time: *10*   Minutes

INGREDIENTS

- ¼ cup oats
- ¼ cup milk
- ½ cup yogurt
- 1 tsp vanilla extract
- 1 tsp honey

DIRECTIONS

1. In a bowl combine all ingredients
2. Refrigerate overnight
3. Serve in the morning

Serves: **2**
Prep Time: **10**   Minutes

Cook Time: **10**   Minutes

Total Time: **20**   Minutes

INGREDIENTS

- 2 scrambled eggs
- 3 oz. salmon
- ½ avocado

DIRECTIONS

1. Scramble eggs and transfer to a plate
2. Add salmon, avocado slices and serve

Serves: **2**

Prep Time: **10**   Minutes

Cook Time: **50**   Minutes

Total Time: **60**   Minutes

INGREDIENTS

- ½ tsp cinnamon
- 1 tsp canola oil
- 1 tablespoon oats
- 1 tsp sugar
- 2 apples

DIRECTIONS

1. Preheat the oven to 325 F
2. In a bowl mix sugar, cinnamon, oats and oil
3. Stuff into cored apples and bake for 40-50 minutes
4. Remove and serve

GREEK OMELET

Serves: **2**

Prep Time: **5**   Minutes

Cook Time: **10**   Minutes

Total Time: **15**   Minutes

INGREDIENTS

- 3 eggs
- ½ cup parsley
- ¼ tsp salt
- ¼ tsp ground pepper
- 1 tsp olive oil
- ¼ cup spinach
- 1 plum tomato
- ½ cup feta cheese
- 6 pitted Kalamata olives

DIRECTIONS

1. In a bowl whisk together eggs, parsley, pepper and salt
2. In a skillet add egg mixture and sprinkle remaining ingredients
3. Cook for 2-3 minutes per side
4. When ready, remove and serve

FRENCH TOAST

Serves: **2**

Prep Time: **10** Minutes

Cook Time: **10** Minutes

Total Time: **20** Minutes

INGREDIENTS

- ½ cup peanut butter
- 2 bread slices
- 2 eggs
- ¼ cup almond milk
- 1 tsp vanilla extract
- 1 tablespoon sugar

DIRECTIONS

1. In a bowl whisk together eggs, vanilla extract, sugar and almond milk
2. Spread peanut butter over bread slices and top with bread slices
3. Dip each sandwich in egg mixture
4. Place sandwiches in a pan and cook for 5-6 minutes per side or until golden brown
5. When ready, remove and serve

ORANGE MUFFINS

Serves: **6**

Prep Time: **10**   Minutes

Cook Time: **20**   Minutes

Total Time: **30**   Minutes

INGREDIENTS

- 1 cup flour
- ¼ cup sugar
- 1 tsp baking powder
- ¼ tsp salt
- 2 eggs
- ¼ cup almond milk
- ½ cup butter
- 1 tsp grated orange rind

DIRECTIONS

1. Preheat oven to 375 F
2. In a bowl mix flour, sugar, salt and baking powder
3. Stir together almond, butter, eggs and dry ingredients and mix well
4. Spoon batter into muffin cups and bake for 18-20 ur until golden brown, remove and serve

BLUEBERRY MUFFINS

Serves: **4**

Prep Time: **10** Minutes

Cook Time: **20** Minutes

Total Time: **30** Minutes

INGREDIENTS

- 2 cups flour
- ½ cup sugar
- 1 tablespoon baking powder
- ¼ tsp salt
- 1 cup almond milk
- ½ cup butter
- 1 egg
- 1 cup blueberries
- 1 cup powdered sugar
- 1 tablespoon lemon juice

DIRECTIONS

1. Preheat the oven to 375 F
2. In a bowl place baking powder, salt, milk, butter and mix well
3. Stir together butter, milk and egg and mix well
4. Add dry ingredients, berries and mix again

5. Spoon batter into muffin cuts and bake for 18-20 minutes or until golden brown

6. When ready, remove and serve

Serves: *1*

Prep Time: *10*   Minutes

Cook Time: *10*   Minutes

Total Time: *20*   Minutes

INGREDIENTS

- 6 eggs
- ½ cup low fat milk
- ¼ tsp salt
- ¼ tsp pepper
- 1 tablespoon butter
- ½ cup cream cheese
- ½ cup Parmesan cheese

DIRECTIONS

1. In a bowl whisk together eggs, salt, milk and pepper
2. In a skillet pour egg mixture and sprinkle cream cheese and cook for 2-3 minutes per side
3. Remove and serve with parmesan cheese

EASY SUNDAY MORNING BAKED EGGS

Serves: 2
Prep Time: 5   Minutes

Cook Time: 25   Minutes

Total Time: 30   Minutes

INGREDIENTS

- 2 Tsp butter
- ¼ shredded red cabbage
- 5 eggs
- ¼ Tsp black pepper
- 1 Tsp grated Parmesan cheese
- 6 cherry tomatoes
- 7 basil leaves

DIRECTIONS

1. Preheat the oven to 400F
2. Divide the butter and place it in the oven until is melted.
3. Sprinkle the cabbage, basil and the tomatoes and crack two eggs into the ramekins.
4. Bake to the desired level of doneness.
5. Sprinkle with Parmesan cheese and black pepper.

Serves: **4**
Prep Time: **10**   Minutes

Cook Time: **10**   Minutes

Total Time: **10**   Minutes

INGREDIENTS

- 1 lb. ground turkey
- 1 tsp sage
- ½ tsp. salt
- ¼ tsp garlic
- dash white pepper
- dash cayenne pepper
- dash ground nutmeg

DIRECTIONS

1. In a bowl mix all ingredients together
2. Form into patties and cook for 2-3 minutes per side or until golden brown
3. Remove and serve

BLUEBERRY PANCAKES

Serves: **4**

Prep Time: **10** Minutes

Cook Time: **20** Minutes

Total Time: **30** Minutes

INGREDIENTS

- 1 cup whole wheat flour
- ¼ tsp baking soda
- ¼ tsp baking powder
- 1 cup blueberries
- 2 eggs
- 1 cup milk

DIRECTIONS

1. In a bowl combine all ingredients together and mix well
2. In a skillet heat olive oil
3. Pour ¼ of the batter and cook each pancake for 1-2 minutes per side
4. When ready remove from heat and serve

Serves: **4**
Prep Time: **10**   Minutes

Cook Time: **30**   Minutes

Total Time: **40**   Minutes

INGREDIENTS

- 1 cup whole wheat flour
- ¼ tsp baking soda
- ¼ tsp baking powder
- 1 cup artichoke
- 2 eggs
- 1 cup milk

DIRECTIONS

1. In a bowl combine all ingredients together and mix well
2. In a skillet heat olive oil
3. Pour ¼ of the batter and cook each pancake for 1-2 minutes per side
4. When ready remove from heat and serve

Serves: **4**
Prep Time: **10** Minutes

Cook Time: **20** Minutes

Total Time: **30** Minutes

INGREDIENTS

- 1 cup whole wheat flour
- ¼ tsp baking soda
- ¼ tsp baking powder
- 1 cup mashed banana
- 2 eggs
- 1 cup milk

DIRECTIONS

1. In a bowl combine all ingredients together and mix well
2. In a skillet heat olive oil
3. Pour ¼ of the batter and cook each pancake for 1-2 minutes per side
4. When ready remove from heat and serve

STRAWBERRY MUFFINS

Serves: *8-12*
Prep Time: *10*   Minutes
Cook Time: *20*   Minutes
Total Time: *30*   Minutes

INGREDIENTS

- 2 eggs
- 1 tablespoon olive oil
- 1 cup milk
- 2 cups whole wheat flour
- 1 tsp baking soda
- ¼ tsp baking soda
- 1 tsp cinnamon
- 1 cup strawberries

DIRECTIONS

1. In a bowl combine all wet ingredients
2. In another bowl combine all dry ingredients
3. Combine wet and dry ingredients together
4. Fold in strawberries and mix well
5. Pour mixture into 8-12 prepared muffin cups, fill 2/3 of the cups
6. Bake for 18-20 minutes at 375 F

COCONUT MUFFINS

Serves: **8-12**

Prep Time: **10**   Minutes

Cook Time: **20**   Minutes

Total Time: **30**   Minutes

INGREDIENTS

- 2 eggs
- 1 tablespoon olive oil
- 1 cup milk
- 2 cups whole wheat flour
- 1 tsp baking soda
- ¼ tsp baking soda
- 1 tsp cinnamon
- 1 cup coconut flakes

DIRECTIONS

1. In a bowl combine all wet ingredients
2. In another bowl combine all dry ingredients
3. Combine wet and dry ingredients together
4. Pour mixture into 8-12 prepared muffin cups, fill 2/3 of the cups
5. Bake for 18-20 minutes at 375 F
6. When ready remove from the oven and serve

CARROT MUFFINS

Serves: **8-12**
Prep Time: **10**   Minutes
Cook Time: **20**   Minutes
Total Time: **30**   Minutes

INGREDIENTS

- 2 eggs
- 1 tablespoon olive oil
- 1 cup milk
- 2 cups whole wheat flour
- 1 tsp baking soda
- ¼ tsp baking soda
- 1 cut carrot
- 1 tsp cinnamon

DIRECTIONS

1. In a bowl combine all wet ingredients
2. In another bowl combine all dry ingredients
3. Combine wet and dry ingredients together
4. Pour mixture into 8-12 prepared muffin cups, fill 2/3 of the cups
5. Bake for 18-20 minutes at 375 F
6. When ready remove from the oven and serve

BEANS OMELETTE

Serves: *1*

Prep Time: 5   Minutes

Cook Time: **10**   Minutes

Total Time: **15**   Minutes

INGREDIENTS

- 2 eggs
- ¼ tsp salt
- ¼ tsp black pepper
- 1 tablespoon olive oil
- ¼ cup cheese
- ¼ tsp basil
- 1 cup beans

DIRECTIONS

1. In a bowl combine all ingredients together and mix well
2. In a skillet heat olive oil and pour the egg mixture
3. Cook for 1-2 minutes per side
4. When ready remove omelette from the skillet and serve

CABBAGE OMELETTE

Serves: *1*

Prep Time: *5*   Minutes

Cook Time: *10*   Minutes

Total Time: *15*   Minutes

INGREDIENTS

- 2 eggs
- ¼ tsp salt
- ¼ tsp black pepper
- 1 tablespoon olive oil
- ¼ cup cheese
- ¼ tsp basil
- 1 cup red onion
- 1 cup cabbage

DIRECTIONS

1. In a bowl combine all ingredients together and mix well
2. In a skillet heat olive oil and pour the egg mixture
3. Cook for 1-2 minutes per side
4. When ready remove omelette from the skillet and serve

Serves: *1*
Prep Time: 5   Minutes

Cook Time: *10*   Minutes

Total Time: *15*   Minutes

INGREDIENTS

- 2 eggs
- ¼ tsp salt
- ¼ tsp black pepper
- 1 tablespoon olive oil
- ¼ cup cheese
- ¼ tsp basil
- 1 cup mushrooms

DIRECTIONS

1. In a bowl combine all ingredients together and mix well
2. In a skillet heat olive oil and pour the egg mixture
3. Cook for 1-2 minutes per side
4. When ready remove omelette from the skillet and serve

TOMATO OMELETTE

Serves: *1*
Prep Time: *5*   Minutes

Cook Time: *10*   Minutes

Total Time: *15*   Minutes

INGREDIENTS

- 2 eggs
- ¼ tsp salt
- ¼ tsp black pepper
- 1 tablespoon olive oil
- ¼ cup cheese
- ¼ tsp basil
- 1 cup tomatoes

DIRECTIONS

1. In a bowl combine all ingredients together and mix well
2. In a skillet heat olive oil and pour the egg mixture
3. Cook for 1-2 minutes per side
4. When ready remove omelette from the skillet and serve

HAZELNUT TART

Serves: *6-8*
Prep Time: **25**   Minutes

Cook Time: **25**   Minutes

Total Time: *50*   Minutes

INGREDIENTS

- pastry sheets
- 3 oz. brown sugar
- ¼ lb. hazelnuts
- 100 ml double cream
- 2 tablespoons syrup
- ¼ lb. dark chocolate
- 2 oz. butter

DIRECTIONS

1. Preheat oven to 400 F, unfold pastry sheets and place them on a baking sheet
2. Toss together all ingredients together and mix well
3. Spread mixture in a single layer on the pastry sheets

4. Before baking decorate with your desired fruits
5. Bake at 400 F for 22-25 minutes or until golden brown
6. When ready remove from the oven and serve

PEAR TART

Serves: **6-8**
Prep Time: **25**   Minutes

Cook Time: **25**   Minutes

Total Time: **50**   Minutes

INGREDIENTS

- 1 lb. pears
- 2 oz. brown sugar
- ½ lb. flaked almonds
- ¼ lb. porridge oat
- 2 oz. flour
- ¼ lb. almonds
- pastry sheets
- 2 tablespoons syrup

DIRECTIONS

1. Preheat oven to 400 F, unfold pastry sheets and place them on a baking sheet
2. Toss together all ingredients together and mix well
3. Spread mixture in a single layer on the pastry sheets
4. Before baking decorate with your desired fruits
5. Bake at 400 F for 22-25 minutes or until golden brown
6. When ready remove from the oven and serve

CARDAMOM TART

Serves: *6-8*
Prep Time: 25   Minutes

Cook Time: 25   Minutes

Total Time: *50*   Minutes

INGREDIENTS

- 4-5 pears
- 2 tablespoons lemon juice
- pastry sheets

CARDAMOM FILLING

- ½ lb. butter
- ½ lb. brown sugar
- ½ lb. almonds
- ¼ lb. flour
- 1 ¼ tsp cardamom
- 2 eggs

DIRECTIONS

1. Preheat oven to 400 F, unfold pastry sheets and place them on a baking sheet
2. Toss together all ingredients together and mix well
3. Spread mixture in a single layer on the pastry sheets
4. Before baking decorate with your desired fruits

5. Bake at 400 F for 22-25 minutes or until golden brown
6. When ready remove from the oven and serve

APPLE TART

Serves: **6-8**
Prep Time: **25**   Minutes

Cook Time: **25**   Minutes

Total Time: **50**   Minutes

INGREDIENTS

- pastry sheets

FILLING

- 1 tsp lemon juice
- 3 oz. brown sugar
- 1 lb. apples
- 150 ml double cream
- 2 eggs

DIRECTIONS

1. Preheat oven to 400 F, unfold pastry sheets and place them on a baking sheet
2. Toss together all ingredients together and mix well
3. Spread mixture in a single layer on the pastry sheets
4. Before baking decorate with your desired fruits
5. Bake at 400 F for 22-25 minutes or until golden brown
6. When ready remove from the oven and serve

PEACH PECAN PIE

Serves: **8-12**

Prep Time: **15**   Minutes
Cook Time: **35**   Minutes
Total Time: **50**   Minutes

INGREDIENTS

- 4-5 cups peaches
- 1 tablespoon preserves
- 1 cup sugar
- 4 small egg yolks
- ¼ cup flour
- 1 tsp vanilla extract

DIRECTIONS

1. Line a pie plate or pie form with pastry and cover the edges of the plate depending on your preference
2. In a bowl combine all pie ingredients together and mix well
3. Pour the mixture over the pastry
4. Bake at 400-425 F for 25-30 minutes or until golden brown
5. When ready remove from the oven and let it rest for 15 minutes

OREO PIE

Serves: **8-12**

Prep Time: **15**   Minutes

Cook Time: **35**   Minutes

Total Time: **50**   Minutes

INGREDIENTS

- pastry sheets
- 6-8 oz. chocolate crumb piecrust
- 1 cup half-and-half
- 1 package instant pudding mix
- 10-12 Oreo cookies
- 10 oz. whipped topping

DIRECTIONS

1. Line a pie plate or pie form with pastry and cover the edges of the plate depending on your preference
2. In a bowl combine all pie ingredients together and mix well
3. Pour the mixture over the pastry
4. Bake at 400-425 F for 25-30 minutes or until golden brown
5. When ready remove from the oven and let it rest for 15 minutes

GRAPEFRUIT PIE

Serves: **8-12**

Prep Time: **15**   Minutes

Cook Time: **35**   Minutes

Total Time: **50**   Minutes

INGREDIENTS

- pastry sheets
- 2 cups grapefruit
- 1 cup brown sugar
- ¼ cup flour
- 5-6 egg yolks
- 5 oz. butter

DIRECTIONS

1. Line a pie plate or pie form with pastry and cover the edges of the plate depending on your preference
2. In a bowl combine all pie ingredients together and mix well
3. Pour the mixture over the pastry
4. Bake at 400-425 F for 25-30 minutes or until golden brown
5. When ready remove from the oven and let it rest for 15 minutes

BUTTERFINGER PIE

Serves: *8-12*
Prep Time: *15*   Minutes
Cook Time: *35*   Minutes
Total Time: *50*   Minutes

INGREDIENTS

- pastry sheets
- 1 package cream cheese
- 1 tsp vanilla extract
- ¼ cup peanut butter
- 1 cup powdered sugar (to decorate)
- 2 cups Butterfinger candy bars
- 8 oz whipped topping

DIRECTIONS

1. Line a pie plate or pie form with pastry and cover the edges of the plate depending on your preference
2. In a bowl combine all pie ingredients together and mix well
3. Pour the mixture over the pastry
4. Bake at 400-425 F for 25-30 minutes or until golden brown
5. When ready remove from the oven and let it rest for 15 minutes

SMOOTHIE RECIPES

WATERMELON SMOOTHIE

Serves: **1**
Prep Time: **5**   Minutes

Cook Time: **5**   Minutes

Total Time: **10** Minutes

INGREDIENTS

- 2 cups watermelon
- 1 cup almond milk
- 1 cup vanilla yogurt
- 2 tablespoons maple syrup
- 1 cup ice

DIRECTIONS

1. In a blender place all ingredients and blend until smooth
2. Pour smoothie in a glass and serve

COCONUT SMOOTHIE

Serves: *1*

Prep Time: 5   Minutes

Cook Time: 5   Minutes

Total Time: *10*   Minutes

INGREDIENTS

- 2 cup pineapple
- ¼ cup coconut milk
- 1 cup pineapple juice
- 2 tablespoons coconut flakes
- ½ cup yogurt
- 1 tablespoon honey

DIRECTIONS

1. In a blender place all ingredients and blend until smooth
2. Pour smoothie in a glass and serve

STRAWBERRY BANANA SMOOTHIE

Serves: *1*

Prep Time: 5   Minutes

Cook Time: 5   Minutes

Total Time: *10*   Minutes

INGREDIENTS

- 1 cup raspberries
- 1 cup strawberries
- 1 banana
- 1 cup almond milk
- 1 tablespoon honey
- 1 cup ice

DIRECTIONS

1. In a blender place all ingredients and blend until smooth
2. Pour smoothie in a glass and serve

Serves: **1**

Prep Time: **5**   Minutes

Cook Time: **5**   Minutes

Total Time: **10**   Minutes

INGREDIENTS

- 1 apple
- 1 pear
- 1 cup coconut water
- 1 tablespoon honey

DIRECTIONS

1. In a blender place all ingredients and blend until smooth
2. Pour smoothie in a glass and serve

GREEN SMOOTHIE

Serves: **1**
Prep Time: 5   Minutes

Cook Time: 5   Minutes

Total Time: **10**   Minutes

INGREDIENTS

- 1 avocado
- 1 cup spinach
- 1 banana
- ½ cup cauliflower
- 2 dates
- 1 cup almond milk

DIRECTIONS

1. In a blender place all ingredients and blend until smooth
2. Pour smoothie in a glass and serve

CLASSIC STRAWBERRY SMOOTHIE

Serves: **1**

Prep Time: **5**   Minutes

Cook Time: **5**   Minutes

Total Time: **10**   Minutes

INGREDIENTS

- 1 cup strawberries
- 1 banana
- 1 cup Greek Yogurt
- 1 cup orange juice

DIRECTIONS

1. In a blender place all ingredients and blend until smooth
2. Pour smoothie in a glass and serve

PEANUT BUTTER SMOOTHIE

Serves: *1*
Prep Time: 5   Minutes

Cook Time: 5   Minutes

Total Time: *10* Minutes

INGREDIENTS

- 2 cups banana
- 1 tablespoon flax seeds
- 1 cup almond milk
- 1 tsp vanilla extract
- 2 tablespoon peanut butter

DIRECTIONS

1. In a blender place all ingredients and blend until smooth
2. Pour smoothie in a glass and serve

SPINACH SMOOTHIE

Serves: *1*

Prep Time: 5   Minutes

Cook Time: 5   Minutes

Total Time: *10*   Minutes

INGREDIENTS

- 2 cups banana
- 2 cups strawberries
- 2 cups spinach
- 2 chia seeds

DIRECTIONS

1. In a blender place all ingredients and blend until smooth
2. Pour smoothie in a glass and serve

PISTACHIOS ICE-CREAM

Serves: **6-8**

Prep Time: **15**   Minutes

Cook Time: **15**   Minutes

Total Time: **30**   Minutes

INGREDIENTS

- 4 egg yolks
- 1 cup heavy cream
- 1 cup milk
- 1 cup sugar
- 1 vanilla bean
- 1 tsp almond extract
- 1 cup cherries
- ½ cup pistachios

DIRECTIONS

1. In a saucepan whisk together all ingredients
2. Mix until bubbly
3. Strain into a bowl and cool

4. Whisk in favorite fruits and mix well
5. Cover and refrigerate for 2-3 hours
6. Pour mixture in the ice-cream maker and follow manufacturer instructions
7. Serve when ready

VANILLA ICE-CREAM

Serves: **6-8**

Prep Time: **15** Minutes

Cook Time: **15** Minutes

Total Time: **30** Minutes

INGREDIENTS

- 1 cup milk
- 1 tablespoon cornstarch
- 1 oz. cream cheese
- 1 cup heavy cream
- 1 cup brown sugar
- 1 tablespoon corn syrup
- 1 vanilla bean

DIRECTIONS

1. In a saucepan whisk together all ingredients
2. Mix until bubbly
3. Strain into a bowl and cool
4. Whisk in favorite fruits and mix well
5. Cover and refrigerate for 2-3 hours
6. Pour mixture in the ice-cream maker and follow manufacturer instructions
7. Serve when ready

FOURTH COOKBOOK

SIDE DISHES

OLIVE GARDEN ZUPPA TOSCANA

Serves: **6**

Prep Time: **10**   Minutes

Cook Time: **20**   Minutes

Total Time: **30**   Minutes

INGREDIENTS

- 4 turnips
- 3 kale leaves
- 1 onion
- 3 cloves garlic
- ½ bacon slices
- 1,5 L chicken broth
- 250 ml heavy cream
- 1 tsp salt
- 4 tablespoon parmesan
- 1 serving homemade Italian sausage

DIRECTIONS

1. In a pot cook the bacon and transfer bacon aside
2. In the same pot add sausage and cook for 4-5 minutes
3. Add onion, chicken broth, turnings and cook until tender

4. Add kale, heavy cream, salt and stir
5. Add sausage back sprinkle with parmesan and serve

GLUTEN FREE CORN DOGS

Serves: *8*
Prep Time: *10*   Minutes

Cook Time: *30*   Minutes

Total Time: *40*   Minutes

INGREDIENTS

- 2 hot dog sausages

CORN DOG BATTER

- 2 tablespoons almond flour
- ½ tsp xanthan gum
- ½ tsp salt
- ½ tsp baking soda
- ¼ tsp baking powder
- ½ tsp garlic powder
- 1 egg
- 1 tablespoon water

DIRECTIONS

1. In a bowl add all ingredients for the corn dogs and whisk together
2. Dip one sausage at a time and roll the skewer
3. Add the corn dog into hot oil and fry for 30 seconds
4. Serve when ready

171

MEATLOAF WITH EGGS

Serves: **6**

Prep Time: **10** Minutes

Cook Time: **50** Minutes

Total Time: **60** Minutes

INGREDIENTS

- ½ onion
- ¼ lb. cabbage
- 3 cloves garlic
- 1 tablespoon olive oil
- ¾ lb. ground chicken
- 1.5 lb. ground pork
- 2 tablespoons parsley
- 1 tsp salt
- 1 tsp black pepper
- 1 tsp mustard
- 1 tablespoon Worcestershire sauce
- 3 boiled eggs

DIRECTIONS

1. Preheat oven to 325 F
2. In a frying pan mix all the veggies cook until soft

3. In a bowl mix ground meat, cooked veggies, parsley and spices
4. Add half the meatloaf mixture to a loaf pan and top with boiled eggs
5. Bake for 40-45 minutes, remove and serve

THAI CHICKEN WINGS

Serves: **5**

Prep Time: **10**   Minutes

Cook Time: **50**   Minutes

Total Time: **60**   Minutes

INGREDIENTS

- 2 lb. chicken drumsticks
- 1 lb. chicken wings
- 1 tablespoon olive oil
- 1 tsp salt
- 1 tsp black pepper
- 4 tablespoons thai sweet chili sauce

DIRECTIONS

1. Preheat the oven to 350 F
2. Add the drumsticks and wings to a baking pan and drizzle the olive oil
3. Sprinkle with salt and pepper all over the wings
4. Bake for 40-45 minutes
5. Remove from the oven and transfer to a frying pan, add thai sweet chili sauce

CHICKEN STIR-FRY

Serves: **6**
Prep Time: **10** Minutes

Cook Time: **20** Minutes

Total Time: **30** Minutes

INGREDIENTS

- 5 chicken breasts
- 2 onions
- 2 bell peppers
- 1 cup broccoli florets
- 1 carrot
- 1 clove garlic
- salt
- 1 tablespoon canola oil
- 2 cups brown rice

DIRECTIONS

1. While rice is cooking, sauté chicken the chicken and set aside
2. Sauté onions, garlic, bell pepper, add carrots and broccoli
3. Add chicken back to skillet, season with salt and pepper
4. Serve with brown rice topped with the chicken mixture

Serves: **4**

Prep Time: **10**   Minutes

Cook Time: **20**   Minutes

Total Time: **30**   Minutes

INGREDIENTS

- 1 can chickpeas
- 1/3 cup water
- 2 tablespoons tahini
- 1 clove garlic
- ½ tsp salt
- 1 tablespoon oil
- 1 tablespoon lemon juice

DIRECTIONS

1. Place all ingredients in a blender and blend until smooth
2. Pour hummus into a container and serve

GRILLED SALMON WITH BASIL

Serves: *4*
Prep Time: *10* Minutes

Cook Time: *20* Minutes

Total Time: *30* Minutes

INGREDIENTS

- 3 salmon steaks
- 2 tablespoons lemon juice
- 2 tablespoons olive oil
- 1 tablespoon basil
- 3 lemon wedges

DIRECTIONS

1. In a bowl mix basil, olive oil, lemon juice and brush both sides of salmon
2. Grill for 10-12 minutes at 150 F
3. Serve with lemon wedges

TUNA MELT

Serves: **2**

Prep Time: **10** Minutes

Cook Time: **10** Minutes

Total Time: **20** Minutes

INGREDIENTS

- 1 can tuna
- 1 whole wheat English muffins
- ½ cup canola mayonnaise
- 3 tomato slices
- 1 tablespoon sweet pickle
- 3 slices cheddar cheese
- ½ tablespoon mustard
- 1 tsp tabasco sauce

DIRECTIONS

1. In a bowl mix sweet pickle, tuna, mayonnaise, mustard and tabasco sauce and mix well
2. Spread tuna mixture on each English muffin
3. Top with tomato and cheddar cheese
4. Broil 4-5 minutes until cheese melts

MOZZARELLA POCKETS

Serves: **2**
Prep Time: **10**   Minutes

Cook Time: **10**   Minutes

Total Time: **20**   Minutes

INGREDIENTS

- 2 whole wheat pita bread rounds
- 2 tomatoes
- 3 tablespoons olive oil
- 3-pieces mozzarella cheese
- 1 garlic clove
- 1 cup basil leaves
- salt

DIRECTIONS

1. Add mozzarella, garlic, basil, tomato and tomato in a bowl and sprinkle with salt, pepper and drizzle with olive oil
2. Place all ingredients in warmed pita pockets

SCRAMBLED EGG SANDWICH

Serves: **2**
Prep Time: **10**   Minutes

Cook Time: **10**   Minutes

Total Time: **20**   Minutes

INGREDIENTS

- 3 slices whole grain bread
- 1 tsp butter
- 1 cloves garlic
- 1 tablespoon dried parsley
- 1 cup egg substitute
- 1 tomato
- ½ tsp salt
- ¼ tsp pepper
- 10 basil leaves
- ½ cup cheddar cheese

DIRECTIONS

1. In a pan melt butter, add garlic, eggs and cook for 2-3 minutes
2. Arrange the egg mixture onto 4 slices of toasted bread
3. Top with basil leaves and sprinkle with cheese

Serves: **6-8**
Prep Time: **10**   Minutes

Cook Time: **15**   Minutes

Total Time: **25**   Minutes

INGREDIENTS

- 1 pizza crust
- 1 tablespoon olive oil
- 6 oz. spinach
- ¼ cup basil
- 1 tsp oregano
- 1 cup mozzarella cheese
- 1 tomato
- ½ cup feta cheese

DIRECTIONS

1. Spread tomato sauce on the pizza crust
2. Place all the toppings on the pizza crust
3. Bake the pizza at 425 F for 12-15 minutes
4. When ready remove pizza from the oven and serve

CHICKEN PIZZA

Serves: **6-8**

Prep Time: **10** Minutes

Cook Time: **15** Minutes

Total Time: **25** Minutes

INGREDIENTS

- 1 cup cooked chicken breast
- ½ cup bbq sauce
- 1 pizza crust
- 1 tablespoon olive oil
- 1 cup cheese
- 1 cup tomatoes

DIRECTIONS

1. Spread tomato sauce on the pizza crust
2. Place all the toppings on the pizza crust
3. Bake the pizza at 425 F for 12-15 minutes
4. When ready remove pizza from the oven and serve

Serves: **6-8**
Prep Time: **10**   Minutes

Cook Time: **15**   Minutes

Total Time: **25**   Minutes

INGREDIENTS

- 1 pizza crust
- 1 tablespoon garlic
- 1 tsp salt
- 2-3 tomatoes
- 1 pizza crust
- 4 oz. mozzarella cheese
- 6-8 basil leaves
- ¼ cup parmesan cheese
- ¼ cup feta cheese

DIRECTIONS

1. Spread tomato sauce on the pizza crust
2. Place all the toppings on the pizza crust
3. Bake the pizza at 425 F for 12-15 minutes
4. When ready remove pizza from the oven and serve

EDAMAME FRITATTA

Serves: **2**

Prep Time: **10** Minutes

Cook Time: **20** Minutes

Total Time: **30** Minutes

INGREDIENTS

- 1 cup edamame
- 1 tablespoon olive oil
- ½ red onion
- 2 eggs
- ¼ tsp salt
- 2 oz. cheddar cheese
- 1 garlic clove
- ¼ tsp dill

DIRECTIONS

1. In a bowl whisk eggs with salt and cheese
2. In a frying pan heat olive oil and pour egg mixture
3. Add remaining ingredients and mix well
4. Serve when ready

PICADILLO

Serves: **3**

Prep Time: **10**   Minutes

Cook Time: **30**   Minutes

Total Time: **40**   Minutes

INGREDIENTS
Sofrito

- 2 tbs olive oil

- 5 oz red bell pepper

- 1 oz garlic

- 7 oz onion

Picadillo

- 5 oz potatoes

- 1 oz raisins

- 1 ½ tsp oregano

- 1/3 cup white wine

- 1 tbs tomato paste

- 1 lb beef

- 7 oz tomatoes

- 2 tsp cumin

- 1 tsp cinnamon

- 1 tsp salt

- 3 oz olives

- 2 tbs olive brine

- 2 bay leaves

DIRECTIONS

1. Sauté the pepper, onions and garlic in oil until tender
2. Add the oregano, cinnamon, bay leaves and cumin and sauté a little bit more
3. Add in the beef, tomato paste, wine, potatoes, tomatoes, raisins, and salt
4. Simmer for about 15 minutes partially covered
5. Add in the olives and let picadillo cook for about 10 minutes
6. Stir in the olive brine when finished
7. Season and serve

CHICKEN STEW

Serves: **2**

Prep Time: **10**   minutes

Cook Time: **30**   minutes

Total Time: **40**   Minutes

INGREDIENTS

- 1/3 cup lime juice
- 1 onion
- 1 ½ cup white wine
- 1/3 cup raisins
- ½ cup oil
- 1 bell pepper
- 1 ½ cup peas
- 1/3 cup orange juice
- 1 lb potatoes
- ¾ cup alcaparrado
- 4 cloves garlic
- 1 can tomato sauce
- Salt
- Pepper
- 1 chicken

DIRECTIONS

1. Mix lime juice, orange juice, chicken, garlic, salt, and pepper
2. Chill for at least 1 hour
3. Cook the marinated chicken for about 10 minutes until browned
4. Cook the pepper and onion until soft, then add wine and cook for another 5 minutes
5. Return the chicken to pan along with the remaining marinade, alcaparrado, tomato sauce, potatoes, ½ cup water, raisins, salt, and pepper.
6. Bring to a boil, then reduce the heat and cook for about 45 minutes
7. Stir in the peas and serve

CHICKEN AND RICE

Serves: **6**
Prep Time: **10**   minutes

Cook Time: **50**   minutes

Total Time: **60**   Minutes

INGREDIENTS

- 3 cloves garlic
- 12 oz diced tomatoes
- 2 tsp cumin
- 3 tsp red pepper flakes
- 4 tbs oil
- 4 cups chicken broth
- 1 tsp saffron
- 3 bay leaves
- 1 tsp salt
- 1/3 tsp black pepper
- 2 ½ lbs chicken
- 2 cups brown rice
- 1 red onion
- 3 bell peppers
- 1 ½ cups green olives
- 3 tbs lime juice

DIRECTIONS

1. Mix the red pepper flakes, lime juice, garlic, salt and pepper
2. Add the chicken and toss to coat
3. Allow to marinate overnight
4. Cook on both sides until golden
5. Warm up the broth and stir in the saffron
6. Saute the onions and peppers until soft.
7. Add in the tomatoes, bay leaves, cumin and rice
8. Cook for about 5 minutes until the juices are absorbed
9. Pour in the broth, add the chicken on top and bring to a boil
10. Reduce the heat and cook covered on low for about 35 minutes
11. Cook uncovered for another 15 minutes
12. Serve topped with cilantro

LOBSTER CREOLE

Serves: *10*
Prep Time: *20*   minutes

Cook Time: *40*   minutes

Total Time: *60*   Minutes

INGREDIENTS

- 6 lobster tails
- 15 oz can crush tomatoes
- 2 lb shrimp
- 1/3 cup olive oil
- 2 onions
- 1 bunch Italian parley
- 1 bay leaf
- 1 cup ketchup
- 2 tsp tabasco
- 1 red pepper
- 5 garlic cloves
- 1 can pimentos
- 2 tbs Worcestershire sauce
- 5 oz tomato sauce
- 1/3 cup wine
- 2 tbs vinegar

- Salt
- Pepper

DIRECTIONS

1. Cut lobster tails into rings and sauté in hot oil until the shells turn red
2. Sauté the onion, garlic, red pepper and bay leaf in the remaining oil for about 10 minutes
3. Stir in the Worcestershire sauce, tomato paste, wine, vinegar, parsley, crushed tomatoes, ketchup, and pimentos
4. Bring to a simmer and cook for 15 minutes, then season with salt and pepper
5. Return the lobster to the pot and simmer for at least 15 minutes
6. Stir in hot sauce
7. Serve immediately

Serves: *8*
Prep Time: *10*   minutes

Cook Time: *60*   minutes

Total Time: *70*   Minutes

INGREDIENTS

- 2 cups rice
- 2 tsp cumin
- 2 tsp fennel
- 1 lb black beans
- 5 cups water
- 1 lb ham
- 3 oregano sprigs
- 3 cloves garlic
- 3 tbs tomato paste
- 1 jalapeno chile
- 3 tbs olive oil
- 2 cups onion
- 2 cups green bell pepper
- 2 ½ tsp salt
- ½ tsp pepper
- 3 bay leaves

DIRECTIONS

1. Rinse the rice and the beans under cold water
2. Place the beans, ham, bay leaves, oregano sprigs, jalapeno and water in a stockpot
3. Bring to a boil, then reduce the heat and simmer for about 40 minutes
4. Pour bean mixture into a colander placed into a bowl, reserving 4 cups liquid
5. Discard jalapenos halves, oregano and bay leaves
6. Remove the ham hock and chop the meat
7. Cook the onion and pepper in hot oil until soft
8. Stir in the cumin, fennel, tomato paste and cook for 5 minutes
9. Add the rice and cook 1 more minute
10. Add ham, black beans, salt, pepper and black beans liquid and bring to a boil
11. Reduce the heat and simmer for 20 minutes
12. Serve immediately

CAULIFLOWER BOWL

Serves: **4**

Prep Time: **10**   minutes

Cook Time: **10**   minutes

Total Time: **20**   Minutes

INGREDIENTS

- 1 sweet potato
- 1 tsp cumin
- 1 tsp oregano
- 4 cloves garlic
- 3 tbs lime juice
- 1/3 cup cilantro
- 5 cups cauliflower florets
- 3 tsp olive oil
- 15 oz black beans
- 1 avocado
- ½ cup pico de gallo
- 3 tsp salt
- 1 tsp black pepper
- 1/3 cup orange juice

DIRECTIONS

1. Mix salt, oil and pepper in a bowl
2. Toss the sweet potatoes in the mixture
3. Roast for at least 10 minutes until tender
4. Mix the lime juice, orange juice, 1 minced garlic clove, 1/3 cup cilantro, oregano, salt, and cumin in a bowl
5. Pulse the cauliflower using a food processor
6. Cook the remaining garlic in hot oil for about half a minute
7. Add the cauliflower, salt, pepper and cook for about 5 minutes
8. Remove from heat and stir in the cilantro
9. Divide among bowls and serve topped with sweet potato, avocado, black beans and pico de gallo

CHICKEN WITH SALSA

Serves: **4**

Prep Time: **15**   Minutes

Cook Time: **15**   Minutes

Total Time: **30**   Minutes

INGREDIENTS
Chicken:
- Pinch chilli flakes
- 1 lb chicken breasts
- 3 tsp garlic granules
- 5 oz grapefruit juice
- 3 tsp cumin
- 2 tsp paprika
- 3 tbs olive oil

Salsa:
- 5 oz grapefruit segments
- 1/3 red onion
- 3 tbs olive oil
- 1 ½ tbs jalapeno pepper
- 3 tbs grapefruit juice
- 2 tbs coriander leaf
- 4 oz jicama

DIRECTIONS

1. Mix the chicken ingredients together except for the chicken breast
2. Place the chicken into the mixture and allow o marinate covered for at least 1 hour
3. Mix the salsa ingredients together in a bowl
4. Cover and refrigerate
5. Grill the chicken for about 5 minutes per side until done
6. Serve with salsa

MEXICAN CHICKEN

Serves: *4*
Prep Time: *10* Minutes

Cook Time: *20* Minutes

Total Time: *30* Minutes

INGREDIENTS

- 2 tsp oil
- 2 chicken breasts
- 2 bell peppers
- 2 cups broccoli florets
- 1 ½ tsp cumin
- 1 tsp cayenne pepper
- 1 tsp paprika

DIRECTIONS

1. Heat a pan
2. Heat the oil for about 20 seconds
3. Add diced chicken and cook for 5 minutes
4. Add the broccoli and peppers and cook for another 10 minutes
5. Add the spices
6. Cook until the water is absorbed

GRILLED SALMON

Serves: **4**

Prep Time: **5** Minutes

Cook Time: **10** Minutes

Total Time: **15** Minutes

INGREDIENTS

- 2 limes juiced
- 1 tbs cilantro
- 1 ½ tsp cumin
- 1 ½ tsp paprika
- 2 lbs salmon
- 1 ½ tbs oil
- 1 tsp onion powder
- 1 tsp chili powder
- 1 avocado
- 2 tsp salt
- 1 red onion

DIRECTIONS

1. Mix the chili powder, onion powder, cumin, paprika, salt and pepper together
2. Rub the salmon with the mix and oil
3. Refrigerate for 30 minutes

4. Preheat the grill

5. Mix the avocado with lime juice, cilantro, and onion together

6. Grill the salmon

7. Serve topped with the avocado salsa

Serves: **8**

Prep Time: **15** Minutes

Cook Time: **4** Hours

Total Time: **4h 15** Minutes

INGREDIENTS

- 1 jalapeno
- 2 cups enchilada sauce
- 1 ½ cup chicken broth
- 1 can black beans
- 2 lb butternut squash
- 1 cup corn
- 1 cup quinoa
- 1 tsp garlic
- 1 can tomatoes

DIRECTIONS

1. Peel and deseed the butternut squash
2. Cut into cubes, then place in the slow cooker
3. Add the corn, quinoa, garlic, tomatoes, black beans, jalapeno, enchilada sauce and the chicken broth
4. Give it a good stir, then cook for 4 hours
5. Allow the liquid to absorb while on low for 30 minutes
6. Season with salt and pepper

ROASTED SQUASH

Serves: **3-4**
Prep Time: **10**   Minutes

Cook Time: **20**   Minutes

Total Time: **30**   Minutes

INGREDIENTS

-   2 delicata squashes
-   2 tablespoons olive oil
-   1 tsp curry powder
-   1 tsp salt

DIRECTIONS

1. Preheat the oven to 400 F
2. Cut everything in half lengthwise
3. Toss everything with olive oil and place onto a prepared baking sheet
4. Roast for 18-20 minutes at 400 F or until golden brown
5. When ready remove from the oven and serve

Serves: **2**
Prep Time: **10** Minutes

Cook Time: **20** Minutes

Total Time: **30** Minutes

INGREDIENTS

- 1 lb. brussels sprouts
- 1 tablespoon olive oil
- 1 tablespoon parmesan cheese
- 1 tsp garlic powder
- 1 tsp seasoning

DIRECTIONS

1. Preheat the oven to 425 F
2. In a bowl toss everything with olive oil and seasoning
3. Spread everything onto a prepared baking sheet
4. Bake for 8-10 minutes or until crisp
5. When ready remove from the oven and serve

ZUCCHINI CHIPS

Serves: *2*

Prep Time: *10*   Minutes

Cook Time: *20*   Minutes

Total Time: *30*   Minutes

INGREDIENTS

- 1 lb. zucchini
- 1 tablespoon olive oil
- 1 tablespoon parmesan cheese
- 1 tsp garlic powder
- 1 tsp seasoning

DIRECTIONS

1. Preheat the oven to 425 F
2. In a bowl toss everything with olive oil and seasoning
3. Spread everything onto a prepared baking sheet
4. Bake for 8-10 minutes or until crisp
5. When ready remove from the oven and serve

CARROT CHIPS

Serves: **2**
Prep Time: **10**   Minutes

Cook Time: **20**   Minutes

Total Time: **30**   Minutes

INGREDIENTS

- 1 lb. carrot
- 1 tablespoon olive oil
- 1 tablespoon parmesan cheese
- 1 tsp garlic powder
- 1 tsp seasoning

DIRECTIONS

1. Preheat the oven to 425 F
2. In a bowl toss everything with olive oil and seasoning
3. Spread everything onto a prepared baking sheet
4. Bake for 8-10 minutes or until crisp
5. When ready remove from the oven and serve

PASTA

SIMPLE SPAGHETTI

Serves: 2
Prep Time: 5   Minutes

Cook Time: 15   Minutes

Total Time: 20   Minutes

INGREDIENTS

- 10 oz. spaghetti
- 2 eggs
- ½ cup parmesan cheese
- 1 tsp black pepper
- Olive oil
- 1 tsp parsley
- 2 cloves garlic

DIRECTIONS

1. In a pot boil spaghetti (or any other type of pasta), drain and set aside
2. In a bowl whish eggs with parmesan cheese
3. In a skillet heat olive oil, add garlic and cook for 1-2 minutes
4. Pour egg mixture and mix well
5. Add pasta and stir well

6. When ready garnish with parsley and serve

CORN PASTA

Serves: 2

Prep Time: 5   Minutes

Cook Time: 15   Minutes

Total Time: 20   Minutes

INGREDIENTS

- 1 lb. pasta
- 4 oz. cheese
- ¼ sour cream
- 1 onion
- 2 cloves garlic
- 1 tsp cumin
- 2 cups corn kernels
- 1 tsp chili powder
- 1 tablespoon cilantro

DIRECTIONS

1. In a pot boil spaghetti (or any other type of pasta), drain and set aside
2. Place all the ingredients for the sauce in a pot and bring to a simmer
3. Add pasta and mix well
4. When ready garnish with parmesan cheese and serve

ARTICHOKE PASTA

Serves: 2

Prep Time: 5   Minutes

Cook Time: 15   Minutes

Total Time: 20   Minutes

INGREDIENTS

- ¼ cup olive oil
- 1 jar artichokes
- 2 cloves garlic
- 1 tablespoon thyme leaves
- 1 lb. pasta
- 2 tablespoons butter
- 1. Cup basil
- ½ cup parmesan cheese

DIRECTIONS

1. In a pot boil spaghetti (or any other type of pasta), drain and set aside
2. Place all the ingredients for the sauce in a pot and bring to a simmer
3. Add pasta and mix well
4. When ready garnish with parmesan cheese and serve

SALAD

SLAW

Serves: **1**

Prep Time: **5** Minutes

Cook Time: **5** Minutes

Total Time: **10** Minutes

INGREDIENTS

- 1 cabbage
- 1 bunch of baby carrots
- ½ cucumber
- 1 bun of cilantro
- 1 bunch of basil
- 1 onion

DIRECTIONS

1. **In a bowl combine all ingredients together and mix well**
2. **Serve with dressing**

Serves: *1*

Prep Time: 5   Minutes

Cook Time: 5   Minutes

Total Time: *10*   Minutes

INGREDIENTS

- 1 egg
- ¼ cup rice vinegar
- 1 tablespoon coconut aminos
- 1 tablespoon sriracha
- 1 tablespoon maple syrup

DIRECTIONS

1. In a bowl combine all ingredients together and mix well
2. Serve with dressing

ARUGULA SALAD

Serves: **1**

Prep Time: **5**   Minutes

Cook Time: **5**   Minutes

Total Time: **10**   Minutes

INGREDIENTS

- 2 cups arugula leaves
- ¼ cup cranberries
- ¼ cup honey
- ¼ cup pecans
- 1 cup salad dressing

DIRECTIONS

1. In a bowl combine all ingredients together and mix well
2. Serve with dressing

Serves: **1**

Prep Time: 5   Minutes

Cook Time: 5   Minutes

Total Time: **10**   Minutes

INGREDIENTS

- ¼ cup masoor
- ¼ cup cucumber
- ½ cup carrot
- ¼ cup tomatoes
- ¼ cup onion

SALAD DRESSING

- ¼ tablespoon olive oil
- 1 tsp lemon juice
- ¼ tsp green chillies
- ½ tsp black pepper

DIRECTIONS

1. In a bowl combine all ingredients together and mix well
2. Add salad dressing, toss well and serve

Serves: *1*
Prep Time: 5   Minutes

Cook Time: 5   Minutes

Total Time: *10* Minutes

INGREDIENTS

- 1 cup muskmelon
- ½ cup pear cubes
- ½ cup apple cubes
- Salad dressing

DIRECTIONS

1. In a bowl combine all ingredients together and mix well
2. Add salad dressing, toss well and serve

CITRUS WATERMELON SALAD

Serves: *1*

Prep Time: *5*   Minutes

Cook Time: *5*   Minutes

Total Time: *10*   Minutes

INGREDIENTS

- 2 cups watermelon
- ¼ cup orange
- ¼ cup sweet lime
- ¼ cup pomegranate

SALAD DRESSING

- 1 tsp olive oil
- 1 tsp lemon juice
- 1 tablespoon parsley

DIRECTIONS

1. In a bowl combine all ingredients together and mix well
2. Add salad dressing, toss well and serve

POTATO SALAD

Serves: **2**
Prep Time: **5**   Minutes

Cook Time: **10**   Minutes

Total Time: **15**   Minutes

INGREDIENTS

- 5 potatoes
- 1 tsp cumin seeds
- 1/3 cup oil
- 2 tsp mustard
- 1 red onion
- 2 cloves garlic
- 1/3 cup lemon juice
- 1 tsp sea salt

DIRECTIONS

1. Steam the potatoes until tender
2. Mix mustard, turmeric powder, lemon juice, cumin seeds, and salt
3. Place the potatoes in a bowl and pour the lemon mixture over
4. Add the chopped onion and minced garlic over
5. Stir to coat and refrigerate covered
6. Add oil and stir before serving

CARROT SALAD

Serves: 2

Prep Time: 5   Minutes

Cook Time: 5   Minutes

Total Time: *10*   Minutes

INGREDIENTS

- 1 ½ tbs lemon juice
- 1/3 tsp salt
- ¼ tsp black pepper
- 2 tbs olive oil
- 1/3 lb carrots
- 1 tsp mustard

DIRECTIONS

1. Mix mustard, lemon juice and oil together
2. Peel and shred the carrots in a bowl
3. Stir in the dressing and season with salt and pepper
4. Mix well and allow to chill for at least 30 minutes

MOROCCAN SALAD

Serves: **2**

Prep Time: **5**   Minutes

Cook Time: **5**   Minutes

Total Time: **10**   Minutes

INGREDIENTS

- 2 tbs lemon juice
- 1 tsp cumin
- 1 tsp paprika
- 3 tbs olive oil
- 2 cloves garlic
- 5 carrots
- Salt
- Pepper

DIRECTIONS

1. Peel and slice the carrots
2. Add the carrots in boiled water and simmer for at least 5 minutes
3. Drain and rinse the carrots under cold water
4. Add in a bowl
5. Mix the lemon juice, garlic, cumin, paprika, and olive oil together

6. Pour the mixture over the carrots and toss then season with salt and pepper

7. Serve immediately

AVOCADO CHICKEN SALAD

Serves: 2

Prep Time: 5   Minutes

Cook Time: 5   Minutes

Total Time: **10**   Minutes

INGREDIENTS

- 3 tsp lime juice
- 3 tbs cilantro
- 1 chicken breast
- 1 avocado
- 1/3 cup onion
- 1 apple
- 1 cup celery
- Salt
- Pepper
- Olive oil

DIRECTIONS

1. Dice the chicken breast
2. Season with salt and pepper and cook into a greased skillet until golden
3. Dice the vegetables and place over the chicken in a bowl
4. Mash the avocado and sprinkle in the cilantro

5. Season with salt and pepper and add lime juice
6. Serve drizzled with olive oil

FIFTH COOKBOOK

BEANS OMELETTE

Serves: **1**

Prep Time: **5**   Minutes

Cook Time: **10**   Minutes

Total Time: **15**   Minutes

INGREDIENTS

- 2 eggs
- ¼ tsp salt
- ¼ tsp black pepper
- 1 tablespoon olive oil
- ¼ cup cheese
- ¼ tsp basil
- 1 cup beans

DIRECTIONS

1. In a bowl combine all ingredients together and mix well
2. In a skillet heat olive oil and pour the egg mixture
3. Cook for 1-2 minutes per side
4. When ready remove omelette from the skillet and serve

BREAKFAST GRANOLA

Serves: 2
Prep Time: 5   Minutes

Cook Time: 30   Minutes

Total Time: 35   Minutes

INGREDIENTS

- 1 tsp vanilla extract
- 1 tablespoon honey
- 1 lb. rolled oats
- 2 tablespoons sesame seeds
- ¼ lb. almonds
- ¼ lb. berries

DIRECTIONS

1. Preheat the oven to 325 F
2. Spread the granola onto a baking sheet
3. Bake for 12-15 minutes, remove and mix everything
4. Bake for another 12-15 minutes or until slightly brown
5. When ready remove from the oven and serve

MANDARIN MUFFINS

Serves: *8-12*
Prep Time: *10*   Minutes

Cook Time: *20*   Minutes

Total Time: *30*   Minutes

INGREDIENTS

- 2 eggs
- 1 tablespoon olive oil
- 1 cup milk
- 2 cups whole wheat flour
- 1 tsp baking soda
- ¼ tsp baking soda
- 1 tsp ginger
- 1 cup mandarin
- ¼ cup molasses

DIRECTIONS

1. In a bowl combine all wet ingredients
2. In another bowl combine all dry ingredients
3. Combine wet and dry ingredients together
4. Pour mixture into 8-12 prepared muffin cups, fill 2/3 of the cups
5. Bake for 18-20 minutes at 375 F

BANANA MUFFINS

Serves: **8-12**

Prep Time: **10** Minutes

Cook Time: **20** Minutes

Total Time: **30** Minutes

INGREDIENTS

- 2 eggs
- 1 tablespoon olive oil
- 1 cup milk
- 2 cups whole wheat flour
- 1 tsp baking soda
- ¼ tsp baking soda
- 1 tsp cinnamon
- 1 cup mashed banana

DIRECTIONS

1. In a bowl combine all wet ingredients
2. In another bowl combine all dry ingredients
3. Combine wet and dry ingredients together
4. Fold in mashed banana and mix well
5. Pour mixture into 8-12 prepared muffin cups, fill 2/3 of the cups
6. Bake for 18-20 minutes at 375 F

POMEGRANATE MUFFINS

Serves: *8-12*

Prep Time: *10*   Minutes

Cook Time: *20*   Minutes

Total Time: *30*   Minutes

INGREDIENTS

- 2 eggs
- 1 tablespoon olive oil
- 1 cup milk
- 2 cups whole wheat flour
- 1 tsp baking soda
- ¼ tsp baking soda
- 1 tsp cinnamon
- 1 cup pomegranate

DIRECTIONS

1. In a bowl combine all wet ingredients
2. In another bowl combine all dry ingredients
3. Combine wet and dry ingredients together
4. Pour mixture into 8-12 prepared muffin cups, fill 2/3 of the cups
5. Bake for 18-20 minutes at 375 F
6. When ready remove from the oven and serve

STRAWBERRY MUFFINS

Serves: **8-12**

Prep Time: **10**   Minutes

Cook Time: **20**   Minutes

Total Time: **30**   Minutes

INGREDIENTS

- 2 eggs
- 1 tablespoon olive oil
- 1 cup milk
- 2 cups whole wheat flour
- 1 tsp baking soda
- ¼ tsp baking soda
- 1 tsp cinnamon
- 1 cup strawberries

DIRECTIONS

1. In a bowl combine all wet ingredients
2. In another bowl combine all dry ingredients
3. Combine wet and dry ingredients together
4. Fold in strawberries and mix well
5. Pour mixture into 8-12 prepared muffin cups, fill 2/3 of the cups
6. Bake for 18-20 minutes at 375 F

PLUMS MUFFINS

Serves: *8-12*
Prep Time: *10*   Minutes

Cook Time: *20*   Minutes

Total Time: *30*   Minutes

INGREDIENTS

-   2 eggs
-   1 tablespoon olive oil
-   1 cup milk
-   2 cups whole wheat flour
-   1 tsp baking soda
-   ¼ tsp baking soda
-   1 tsp cinnamon
-   1 cup plums

DIRECTIONS

1. In a bowl combine all wet ingredients
2. In another bowl combine all dry ingredients
3. Combine wet and dry ingredients together
4. Pour mixture into 8-12 prepared muffin cups, fill 2/3 of the cups
5. Bake for 18-20 minutes at 375 F
6. When ready remove from the oven and serve

ZUCCHINI OMELETTE

Serves: **1**

Prep Time: **5** Minutes

Cook Time: **10** Minutes

Total Time: **15** Minutes

INGREDIENTS

- 2 eggs
- ¼ tsp salt
- ¼ tsp black pepper
- 1 tablespoon olive oil
- ¼ cup cheese
- ¼ tsp basil
- 1 cup zucchini

DIRECTIONS

1. In a bowl combine all ingredients together and mix well
2. In a skillet heat olive oil and pour the egg mixture
3. Cook for 1-2 minutes per side
4. When ready remove omelette from the skillet and serve

BASIL OMELETTE

Serves: **1**
Prep Time: **5**   Minutes
Cook Time: **10**   Minutes
Total Time: **15**   Minutes

INGREDIENTS

- 2 eggs
- ¼ tsp salt
- ¼ tsp black pepper
- 1 tablespoon olive oil
- ¼ cup cheese
- ¼ tsp basil
- 1 cup red onion

DIRECTIONS

1. In a bowl combine all ingredients together and mix well
2. In a skillet heat olive oil and pour the egg mixture
3. Cook for 1-2 minutes per side
4. When ready remove omelette from the skillet and serve

MUSHROOM OMELETTE

Serves: *1*
Prep Time: *5* Minutes

Cook Time: *10* Minutes

Total Time: *15* Minutes

INGREDIENTS

- 2 eggs
- ¼ tsp salt
- ¼ tsp black pepper
- 1 tablespoon olive oil
- ¼ cup cheese
- ¼ tsp basil
- 1 cup mushrooms

DIRECTIONS

1. In a bowl combine all ingredients together and mix well
2. In a skillet heat olive oil and pour the egg mixture
3. Cook for 1-2 minutes per side
4. When ready remove omelette from the skillet and serve

PUMPKIN OMELETTE

Serves: *1*

Prep Time: *5*   Minutes

Cook Time: *10* Minutes

Total Time: *15* Minutes

INGREDIENTS

- 2 eggs
- ¼ tsp salt
- ¼ tsp black pepper
- 1 tablespoon olive oil
- ¼ cup cheese
- ¼ tsp basil
- 1 cup pumpkin puree

DIRECTIONS

1. In a bowl combine all ingredients together and mix well
2. In a skillet heat olive oil and pour the egg mixture
3. Cook for 1-2 minutes per side
4. When ready remove omelette from the skillet and serve

BLUEBERRIES OATMEAL

Serves: *2*
Prep Time: *10*   Minutes

Cook Time: *8*   Hours

Total Time: *8*   Hours

INGREDIENTS

- 1/3 cup oats
- 1/3 cup blueberries
- 2 tbs maple syrup
- 1/3 cup coconut milk
- ½ tsp vanilla
- 1 banana
- 1 ½ tsp chia seeds

DIRECTIONS

1. Mix the oats and chia seeds together
2. Pour in the milk and top with blueberries and sliced banana
3. Refrigerate for at least 8 hours
4. Stir in the maple syrup and serve

CHIA PUDDING

Serves: 2

Prep Time: 5   Minutes

Cook Time: 10   Minutes

Total Time: 15   Minutes

INGREDIENTS

- 5 tbs chia seeds
- 1 ½ tbs vanilla
- 2 tbs maple syrup
- 2 ½ cup almond milk
- 1 ½ cup strawberries
- 1 beet

DIRECTIONS

1. Blend together the milk, strawberries, chopped beet, maple syrup, and vanilla
2. Pour into a cup and ad the chia
3. Stir every 5 minutes for 15 minutes
4. Refrigerate overnight
5. Serve topped with fruits

BREAKFAST CASSEROLE

Serves: **4**
Prep Time: **10**   Minutes

Cook Time: **35**   Minutes

Total Time: **45**   Minutes

INGREDIENTS

- 7 oz asparagus
- 3 tbs parsley
- 1 cup broccoli
- 1 zucchini
- 3 tbs oil
- 5 eggs
- Salt
- Pepper

DIRECTIONS

1. Cook the diced zucchini, asparagus and broccoli florets in heated oil for about 5 minutes
2. Season with salt and pepper and remove from heat
3. Whisk the eggs and season then add the parsley
4. Place the vegetables in a greased pan then pour the eggs over
5. Bake in the preheated oven for about 35 minutes at 350F

BLUEBERRY BALLS

Serves: *12*

Prep Time: *5*   Minutes

Cook Time: *30* Minutes

Total Time: *35* Minutes

INGREDIENTS

- 2 cups oats
- 1 cup blueberries
- 1/3 cup honey
- 1 tsp cinnamon
- 1 ½ tsp vanilla
- 1/3 cup almond butter

DIRECTIONS

1. Mix the honey, vanilla, oats, almond butter, and cinnamon together
2. Fold in the blueberries
3. Refrigerate for at least 30 minutes
4. Form balls from the dough and serve

ZUCCHINI BREAD

Serves: **4**

Prep Time: **10** Minutes

Cook Time: **40** Minutes

Total Time: **50** Minutes

INGREDIENTS

- 4 tbs honey
- 5 tbs oil
- 1 ½ tsp baking soda
- 3 eggs
- ½ cup walnuts
- 2 ½ cups flour
- 4 Medjool dates
- 1 banana
- 2 tsp mixed spice
- 1 ½ cup zucchini

DIRECTIONS

1. Preheat the oven to 350 F
2. Chop the dates and the walnuts
3. Mix the flour, spice and baking soda together
4. Mix the eggs and banana in a food processor then add remaining ingredients and mix

5. Pour the batter into a pan and cook for at least 40 minutes
6. Allow to cool then serve

Serves: **4**
Prep Time: **10** Minutes

Cook Time: **20** Minutes

Total Time: **30** Minutes

INGREDIENTS

- 1 cup whole wheat flour
- ¼ tsp baking soda
- ¼ tsp baking powder
- 1 cup blueberries
- 2 eggs
- 1 cup milk

DIRECTIONS

1. In a bowl combine all ingredients together and mix well
2. In a skillet heat olive oil
3. Pour ¼ of the batter and cook each pancake for 1-2 minutes per side
4. When ready remove from heat and serve

NECTARINE PANCAKES

Serves: *4*

Prep Time: *10* Minutes

Cook Time: *30* Minutes

Total Time: *40* Minutes

INGREDIENTS

- 1 cup whole wheat flour
- ¼ tsp baking soda
- ¼ tsp baking powder
- 1 cup nectarine
- 2 eggs
- 1 cup milk

DIRECTIONS

1. In a bowl combine all ingredients together and mix well
2. In a skillet heat olive oil
3. Pour ¼ of the batter and cook each pancake for 1-2 minutes per side
4. When ready remove from heat and serve

BANANA PANCAKES

Serves: **4**

Prep Time: **10** Minutes

Cook Time: **20** Minutes

Total Time: **30** Minutes

INGREDIENTS

- 1 cup whole wheat flour
- ¼ tsp baking soda
- ¼ tsp baking powder
- 1 cup mashed banana
- 2 eggs
- 1 cup milk

DIRECTIONS

1. In a bowl combine all ingredients together and mix well
2. In a skillet heat olive oil
3. Pour ¼ of the batter and cook each pancake for 1-2 minutes per side
4. When ready remove from heat and serve

ONION PANCAKES

Serves: **4**

Prep Time: **10** Minutes

Cook Time: **20** Minutes

Total Time: **30** Minutes

INGREDIENTS

- 1 cup whole wheat flour
- ¼ tsp baking soda
- ¼ tsp baking powder
- 1 cup onion
- 2 eggs
- 1 cup milk

DIRECTIONS

1. In a bowl combine all ingredients together and mix well
2. In a skillet heat olive oil
3. Pour ¼ of the batter and cook each pancake for 1-2 minutes per side
4. When ready remove from heat and serve

PANCAKES

Serves: *4*
Prep Time: *10* Minutes

Cook Time: *30* Minutes

Total Time: *40* Minutes

INGREDIENTS

- 1 cup whole wheat flour
- ¼ tsp baking soda
- ¼ tsp baking powder
- 2 eggs
- 1 cup milk

DIRECTIONS

1. In a bowl combine all ingredients together and mix well
2. In a skillet heat olive oil
3. Pour ¼ of the batter and cook each pancake for 1-2 minutes per side
4. When ready remove from heat and serve

Serves: *1*
Prep Time: 5   Minutes

Cook Time: 5   Minutes

Total Time: *10*   Minutes

INGREDIENTS

- ½ cup dried raisins
- ½ cup dried pecans
- ¼ cup almonds
- 1 cup coconut milk
- 1 tsp cinnamon

DIRECTIONS

1. In a bowl combine all ingredients together
2. Serve with milk

SAUSAGE BREAKFAST SANDWICH

Serves: 2
Prep Time: 5   Minutes

Cook Time: 15   Minutes

Total Time: 20   Minutes

INGREDIENTS

- ¼ cup egg substitute
- 1 muffin
- 1 turkey sausage patty
- 1 tablespoon cheddar cheese

DIRECTIONS

1. In a skillet pour egg and cook on low heat
2. Place turkey sausage patty in a pan and cook for 4-5 minutes per side
3. On a toasted muffin place the cooked egg, top with a sausage patty and cheddar cheese
4. Serve when ready

STRAWBERRY MUFFINS

Serves: **8-12**

Prep Time: **10** Minutes

Cook Time: **20** Minutes

Total Time: **30** Minutes

INGREDIENTS

- 2 eggs
- 1 tablespoon olive oil
- 1 cup milk
- 2 cups whole wheat flour
- 1 tsp baking soda
- ¼ tsp baking soda
- 1 tsp cinnamon
- 1 cup strawberries

DIRECTIONS

1. In a bowl combine all wet ingredients
2. In another bowl combine all dry ingredients
3. Combine wet and dry ingredients together
4. Pour mixture into 8-12 prepared muffin cups, fill 2/3 of the cups
5. Bake for 18-20 minutes at 375 F
6. When ready remove from the oven and serve

DESSERTS

BREAKFAST COOKIES

Serves: *8-12*
Prep Time: 5   Minutes

Cook Time: *15*   Minutes

Total Time: *20*   Minutes

INGREDIENTS

- 1 cup rolled oats
- ¼ cup applesauce
- ½ tsp vanilla extract
- 3 tablespoons chocolate chips
- 2 tablespoons dried fruits
- 1 tsp cinnamon

DIRECTIONS

1. Preheat the oven to 325 F
2. In a bowl combine all ingredients together and mix well
3. Scoop cookies using an ice cream scoop
4. Place cookies onto a prepared baking sheet
5. Place in the oven for 12-15 minutes or until the cookies are done
6. When ready remove from the oven and serve

PEAR TART

Serves: *6-8*
Prep Time: *25*   Minutes

Cook Time: *25*   Minutes

Total Time: *50*   Minutes

INGREDIENTS

- 1 lb. pears
- 2 oz. brown sugar
- ½ lb. flaked almonds
- ¼ lb. porridge oat
- 2 oz. flour
- ¼ lb. almonds
- pastry sheets
- 2 tablespoons syrup

DIRECTIONS

1. Preheat oven to 400 F, unfold pastry sheets and place them on a baking sheet
2. Toss together all ingredients together and mix well
3. Spread mixture in a single layer on the pastry sheets
4. Before baking decorate with your desired fruits
5. Bake at 400 F for 22-25 minutes or until golden brown
6. When ready remove from the oven and serve

CARDAMOM TART

Serves: **6-8**

Prep Time: **25** Minutes

Cook Time: **25** Minutes

Total Time: **50** Minutes

INGREDIENTS

- 4-5 pears
- 2 tablespoons lemon juice
- pastry sheets

CARDAMOM FILLING

- ½ lb. butter
- ½ lb. brown sugar
- ½ lb. almonds
- ¼ lb. flour
- 1 ¼ tsp cardamom
- 2 eggs

DIRECTIONS

1. Preheat oven to 400 F, unfold pastry sheets and place them on a baking sheet
2. Toss together all ingredients together and mix well
3. Spread mixture in a single layer on the pastry sheets
4. Before baking decorate with your desired fruits

5. Bake at 400 F for 22-25 minutes or until golden brown
6. When ready remove from the oven and serve

APPLE TART

Serves: **6-8**
Prep Time: **25**   Minutes

Cook Time: **25**   Minutes

Total Time: **50**   Minutes

INGREDIENTS

- pastry sheets

FILLING

- 1 tsp lemon juice
- 3 oz. brown sugar
- 1 lb. apples
- 150 ml double cream
- 2 eggs

DIRECTIONS

1. Preheat oven to 400 F, unfold pastry sheets and place them on a baking sheet
2. Toss together all ingredients together and mix well
3. Spread mixture in a single layer on the pastry sheets
4. Before baking decorate with your desired fruits
5. Bake at 400 F for 22-25 minutes or until golden brown
6. When ready remove from the oven and serve

CHOCHOLATE TART

Serves: **6-8**

Prep Time: **25** Minutes

Cook Time: **25** Minutes

Total Time: **50** Minutes

INGREDIENTS

- pastry sheets
- 1 tsp vanilla extract
- ½ lb. caramel
- ½ lb. black chocolate
- 4-5 tablespoons butter
- 3 eggs
- ¼ lb. brown sugar

DIRECTIONS

1. Preheat oven to 400 F, unfold pastry sheets and place them on a baking sheet
2. Toss together all ingredients together and mix well
3. Spread mixture in a single layer on the pastry sheets
4. Before baking decorate with your desired fruits
5. Bake at 400 F for 22-25 minutes or until golden brown
6. When ready remove from the oven and serve

OREO PIE

Serves: **8-12**

Prep Time: **15** Minutes

Cook Time: **35** Minutes

Total Time: **50** Minutes

INGREDIENTS

- pastry sheets
- 6-8 oz. chocolate crumb piecrust
- 1 cup half-and-half
- 1 package instant pudding mix
- 10-12 Oreo cookies
- 10 oz. whipped topping

DIRECTIONS

1. Line a pie plate or pie form with pastry and cover the edges of the plate depending on your preference
2. In a bowl combine all pie ingredients together and mix well
3. Pour the mixture over the pastry
4. Bake at 400-425 F for 25-30 minutes or until golden brown
5. When ready remove from the oven and let it rest for 15 minutes

WATERMELON SMOOTHIE

Serves: **1**

Prep Time: **5** Minutes

Cook Time: **5** Minutes

Total Time: **10** Minutes

INGREDIENTS

- 4 cups watermelon
- 4-5 basil leaves
- 1 cup coconut water
- 1 cup ice

DIRECTIONS

1. In a blender place all ingredients and blend until smooth
2. Pour smoothie in a glass and serve

COCONUT SMOOTHIE

Serves: *1*
Prep Time: 5   Minutes

Cook Time: 5   Minutes

Total Time: *10*   Minutes

INGREDIENTS

- 1 cup cherries
- 1 cup coconut water
- 1 tablespoon lime juice
- 2 tablespoons coconut flakes
- 1 cup cherries

DIRECTIONS

1. In a blender place all ingredients and blend until smooth
2. Pour smoothie in a glass and serve

AVOCADO SMOOTHIE

Serves: *1*

Prep Time: *5*   Minutes

Cook Time: *5*   Minutes

Total Time: *10*   Minutes

INGREDIENTS

- 1 avocado
- 1 banana
- 1 cup soy milk
- 1 cup ice

DIRECTIONS

1. In a blender place all ingredients and blend until smooth
2. Pour smoothie in a glass and serve

GREEK SMOOTHIE

Serves: **1**
Prep Time: **5**   Minutes

Cook Time: **5**   Minutes

Total Time: **10** Minutes

INGREDIENTS

- 1 mango
- 3-4 tablespoons Greek yogurt
- 1 tsp cinnamon
- 1 cup ice

DIRECTIONS

1. In a blender place all ingredients and blend until smooth
2. Pour smoothie in a glass and serve

FRUIT SMOOTHIE

Serves: *1*

Prep Time: 5   Minutes

Cook Time: 5   Minutes

Total Time: *10*   Minutes

INGREDIENTS

- 1 cup berries
- 4-5 oz. strawberry yogurt
- 1 cup cashew milk

DIRECTIONS

1. In a blender place all ingredients and blend until smooth
2. Pour smoothie in a glass and serve

PEANUT BUTTER SMOOTHIE

Serves: **1**

Prep Time: **5**   Minutes

Cook Time: **5**   Minutes

Total Time: **10**   Minutes

INGREDIENTS

- 1 banana
- ¼ cup peanut butter
- 1 cup soy milk
- 1 cup ice

DIRECTIONS

1. **In a blender place all ingredients and blend until smooth**
2. **Pour smoothie in a glass and serve**

Serves: *1*
Prep Time: 5 Minutes

Cook Time: 5 Minutes

Total Time: *10* Minutes

INGREDIENTS

- 2 cups pineapple
- ¼ cup mint leaves
- 1 cup coconut water
- 1 cup ice

DIRECTIONS

1. In a blender place all ingredients and blend until smooth
2. Pour smoothie in a glass and serve

BANANA & STRAWBERRY SMOOTHIE

Serves: *1*
Prep Time: 5   Minutes

Cook Time: 5   Minutes

Total Time: *10* Minutes

INGREDIENTS

- 4-5 strawberries
- 1 banana
- 1 cup almond milk

DIRECTIONS

1. In a blender place all ingredients and blend until smooth
2. Pour smoothie in a glass and serve

GREEN SMOOTHIE

Serves: *1*
Prep Time: *5*   Minutes
Cook Time: *5*   Minutes
Total Time: *10*   Minutes

INGREDIENTS

- 1 cup baby spinach
- 1 cup coconut milk
- 1 cup pineapple
- 1 cup ice

DIRECTIONS

1. In a blender place all ingredients and blend until smooth
2. Pour smoothie in a glass and serve

BREAKFAST SMOOTHIE

Serves: **1**

Prep Time: 5 Minutes

Cook Time: 5 Minutes

Total Time: **10** Minutes

INGREDIENTS

- 1 cup kale
- 1 cup almond milk
- 1 cup oats

DIRECTIONS

1. In a blender place all ingredients and blend until smooth
2. Pour smoothie in a glass and serve

SIXTH COOKBOOK

ROASTED JALAPENO SOUP

Serves: *4*

Prep Time: *10*   Minutes

Cook Time: *20*   Minutes

Total Time: *30*   Minutes

INGREDIENTS

- 1 tablespoon olive oil
- 1 tablespoon roasted jalapeno
- ¼ red onion
- ½ cup all-purpose flour
- ¼ tsp salt
- ¼ tsp pepper
- 1 can vegetable broth
- 1 cup heavy cream

DIRECTIONS

1. In a saucepan heat olive oil and sauté onion until tender
2. Add remaining ingredients to the saucepan and bring to a boil
3. When all the vegetables are tender transfer to a blender and blend until smooth
4. Pour soup into bowls, garnish with parsley and serve

PARSNIP SOUP

Serves: **4**

Prep Time: **10**   Minutes

Cook Time: **20**   Minutes

Total Time: **30**   Minutes

INGREDIENTS

- 1 tablespoon olive oil
- 1 cup parsnip
- ¼ red onion
- ½ cup all-purpose flour
- ¼ tsp salt
- ¼ tsp pepper
- 1 can vegetable broth
- 1 cup heavy cream

DIRECTIONS

1. In a saucepan heat olive oil and sauté parsnip until tender
2. Add remaining ingredients to the saucepan and bring to a boil
3. When all the vegetables are tender transfer to a blender and blend until smooth
4. Pour soup into bowls, garnish with parsley and serve

SPINACH SOUP

Serves: **4**
Prep Time: **10**   Minutes

Cook Time: **20**   Minutes

Total Time: **30**   Minutes

INGREDIENTS

- 1 tablespoon olive oil
- 1 lb. spinach
- ¼ red onion
- ½ cup all-purpose flour
- ¼ tsp salt
- ¼ tsp pepper
- 1 can vegetable broth
- 1 cup heavy cream

DIRECTIONS

1. In a saucepan heat olive oil and sauté spinach until tender
2. Add remaining ingredients to the saucepan and bring to a boil
3. When all the vegetables are tender transfer to a blender and blend until smooth
4. Pour soup into bowls, garnish with parsley and serve

CUCUMBER SOUP

Serves: **4**

Prep Time: **10**   Minutes

Cook Time: **20**   Minutes

Total Time: **30**   Minutes

INGREDIENTS

- 1 tablespoon olive oil
- 1 lb. cucumber
- ¼ red onion
- ½ cup all-purpose flour
- ¼ tsp salt
- ¼ tsp pepper
- 1 can vegetable broth
- 1 cup heavy cream

DIRECTIONS

1. In a saucepan heat olive oil and sauté onion until tender
2. Add remaining ingredients to the saucepan and bring to a boil
3. When all the vegetables are tender transfer to a blender and blend until smooth
4. Pour soup into bowls, garnish with parsley and serve

SWEETCORN SOUP

Serves: **4**

Prep Time: **10** Minutes

Cook Time: **20** Minutes

Total Time: **30** Minutes

INGREDIENTS

- 1 tablespoon olive oil
- 1 lb. sweetcorn
- ¼ red onion
- ½ cup all-purpose flour
- ¼ tsp salt
- ¼ tsp pepper
- 1 can vegetable broth
- 1 cup heavy cream

DIRECTIONS

1. In a saucepan heat olive oil and sauté onion until tender
2. Add remaining ingredients to the saucepan and bring to a boil
3. When all the vegetables are tender transfer to a blender and blend until smooth
4. Pour soup into bowls, garnish with parsley and serve

GREEN PESTO PASTA

Serves: **2**

Prep Time: **5**   Minutes

Cook Time: **15**   Minutes

Total Time: **20**   Minutes

INGREDIENTS

- 4 oz. spaghetti
- 2 cups basil leaves
- 2 garlic cloves
- ¼ cup olive oil
- 2 tablespoons parmesan cheese
- ½ tsp black pepper

DIRECTIONS

1. Bring water to a boil and add pasta
2. In a blend add parmesan cheese, basil leaves, garlic and blend
3. Add olive oil, pepper and blend again
4. Pour pesto onto pasta and serve when ready

CHICKEN AND BROCCOLI

Serves: **4**

Prep Time: **5**   Minutes

Cook Time: **10**   Minutes

Total Time: **15**   Minutes

INGREDIENTS

-   1 lb chicken thighs
-   1 ½ tbs sesame seeds
-   2 tsp garlic
-   1/3 cup oyster sauce
-   2 tbs oil
-   1/3 cup chicken broth
-   2 tsp honey
-   1 tsp sesame oil
-   2 cups broccoli florets
-   1 ½ tsp soy sauce
-   1 tsp cornstarch
-   Salt
-   Pepper

DIRECTIONS

1.   Cook the broccoli in hot oil until tender
2.   Add the garlic and cook 30 more seconds

3. Place the seasoned chicken in the pan and cook until browned

4. Mix the oyster sauce, honey, soy sauce, chicken broth and sesame oil together

5. Combine the cornstarch with 1 tbs of cold water

6. Pour the oyster mixture over the chicken and broccoli and cook for 30 seconds

7. Add the cornstarch, bring to a boil and cook for a minute

8. Serve topped with sesame seeds

CHICKEN AND RICE

Serves: *4*

Prep Time: *10*   Minutes

Cook Time: *20*   Minutes

Total Time: *30*   Minutes

INGREDIENTS

- 1 cup rice
- 15 oz salsa
- 3 tsp paprika
- 3 tbs olive oil
- 1 ½ cup chicken broth
- 2 lb chicken thigh

DIRECTIONS

1. Cut the chicken and toss with the paprika
2. Cook in hot oil until browned
3. Add the rice and mix well, cooking 1 more minute to toast the rice
4. Add the broth and salsa and stir
5. Bring to a simmer, then cover and cook for 20 minutes
6. Serve immediately

Serves: **8**
Prep Time: **10** Minutes

Cook Time: **20** Minutes

Total Time: **30** Minutes

INGREDIENTS

- Tortilla shells
- 3 bell peppers
- 2 tbs olive oil
- 2 cups green lentils
- 1 onion
- 3 cloves garlic
- 3 cups mushrooms
- 1 package taco seasoning
- 2 tsp paprika
- 1 cup water
- Parsley

DIRECTIONS

1. Sauté the peppers in hot oil until soft
2. Add the onions and garlic and cook until soft
3. Add the mushrooms, lentils, paprika and taco seasoning and stir until the mushrooms release some juice

4. Add the water slowly to create a sauce
5. Reduce the heat and cook for 15 minutes
6. Add the bell peppers and combine
7. Place the mixture onto each taco shell
8. Serve immediately

BBQ CHICKEN

Serves: **4**

Prep Time: **10** Minutes

Cook Time: 5   Hours

Total Time: **40** Minutes

INGREDIENTS

- 1/3 cup chicken broth
- 1 cup BBQ sauce
- 1 ½ lbs chicken breasts

DIRECTIONS

1. Place the ingredients in a crockpot and cook on low for 5 hours
2. Break the meat to shred
3. Serve over a bun

TUNA MELTS

Serves: **2**

Prep Time: **5** Minutes

Cook Time: **5** Minutes

Total Time: **10** Minutes

INGREDIENTS

- 6 oz tuna
- 3 tbs onion
- ¼ tsp salt
- ¼ tsp black pepper
- 1 avocado
- 3 tbs Greek yogurt
- 3 oz cheese
- 2 tomatoes

DIRECTIONS

1. Mix together onion, tuna, diced avocado, Greek yogurt, salt, and pepper
2. Place tomato slices on a baking sheet on a wire rack
3. To each slice with tuna mixture, then top with cheese
4. Broil until cheese is melted

CAPRESE SALAD

Serves: **2**

Prep Time: **5** Minutes

Cook Time: **5** Minutes

Total Time: **10** Minutes

INGREDIENTS

- 3 cups tomatoes
- 2 oz. mozzarella cheese
- 2 tablespoons basil
- 1 tablespoon olive oil

DIRECTIONS

1. In a bowl combine all ingredients together and mix well
2. Serve with dressing

BUTTERNUT SQUASH SALAD

Serves:	2	
Prep Time:	5	Minutes
Cook Time:	5	Minutes
Total Time:	10	Minutes

INGREDIENTS

- 3 cups butternut squash
- 1 cup cooked couscous
- 2 cups kale leaves
- 2 tablespoons cranberries
- 2 oz. goat cheese
- 1 cup salad dressing

DIRECTIONS

1. In a bowl combine all ingredients together and mix well
2. Serve with dressing

Serves: **2**

Prep Time: **5**   Minutes

Cook Time: **5**   Minutes

Total Time: **10** Minutes

INGREDIENTS

- 2 tablespoons lemon juice
- 2 tablespoons roasted garlic
- 2 tablespoons olive oil
- 1 tablespoon honey
- 2 cups cooked turkey breast
- 1 cup berries
- 1 cup green onions

DIRECTIONS

1. In a bowl combine all ingredients together and mix well
2. Serve with dressing

Serves: **2**

Prep Time: **5**   Minutes

Cook Time: **5**   Minutes

Total Time: **10**   Minutes

INGREDIENTS

- 2 cups watermelon
- 1 cup cantaloupe
- 1 tablespoon honey
- 1 tablespoon mint
- 1 tsp basil leaves
- ½ cup feta cheese

DIRECTIONS

1. In a bowl combine all ingredients together and mix well
2. Serve with dressing

CORN SALAD

Serves: **2**

Prep Time: **5**   Minutes

Cook Time: **5**   Minutes

Total Time: **10** Minutes

INGREDIENTS

- 1 cup corn
- 1 cup cucumber
- 1 cup tomatoes
- ¼ cup avocado
- 1 tablespoon lime juice
- ½ cup Greek yogurt
- 1 cup salad dressing

DIRECTIONS

1. In a bowl combine all ingredients together and mix well
2. Serve with dressing

Serves: **2**
Prep Time: **5**   Minutes
Cook Time: **5**   Minutes
Total Time: **10** Minutes

INGREDIENTS

- 2 hard boiled eggs
- ¼ cup red onion
- 2 tablespoons capers
- 1 tablespoon lime juice
- 3 oz. smoked salmon
- 1 tablespoon olive oil

DIRECTIONS

1. In a bowl combine all ingredients together and mix well
2. Serve with dressing

QUINOA SALAD

Serves: **2**

Prep Time: **5**   Minutes

Cook Time: **5**   Minutes

Total Time: **10** Minutes

INGREDIENTS

- 1 cup cooked quinoa
- 1 tablespoon olive oil
- 1 tablespoon mustard
- 2 tablespoons lemon juice
- 1 cucumber
- ½ red onion
- ½ cup almonds
- 1 tablespoon mint

DIRECTIONS

1. **In a bowl combine all ingredients together and mix well**
2. **Serve with dressing**

GREEK SALAD

Serves: 2
Prep Time: 5   Minutes

Cook Time: 5   Minutes

Total Time: **10**   Minutes

INGREDIENTS

- 1 cup cucumber
- ¼ cup tomatoes
- ¼ cup red onion
- ¼ cup avocado
- ¼ cup feta cheese
- 1 tablespoon olives
- ¼ pecans
- 1 tablespoon vinegar
- 1 tsp olive oil

DIRECTIONS

1. In a bowl combine all ingredients together and mix well
2. Serve with dressing

AVOCADO SALAD

Serves: **2**

Prep Time: **5**   Minutes

Cook Time: **5**   Minutes

Total Time: **10**   Minutes

INGREDIENTS

- 1 cup corn
- 1 cup tomatoes
- 1 cup cucumber
- ½ cup avocado
- ½ cup edamame
- 1 cup salad dressing

DIRECTIONS

1. In a bowl combine all ingredients together and mix well
2. Serve with dressing

ENDIVE FRITATTA

Serves: **2**
Prep Time: **10** Minutes

Cook Time: **20** Minutes

Total Time: **30** Minutes

INGREDIENTS

- ½ lb. endive
- 1 tablespoon olive oil
- ½ red onion
- 2 eggs
- ¼ tsp salt
- 2 oz. cheddar cheese
- 1 garlic clove
- ¼ tsp dill

DIRECTIONS

1. In a bowl whisk eggs with salt and cheese
2. In a frying pan heat olive oil and pour egg mixture
3. Add remaining ingredients and mix well
4. Serve when ready

Serves: **2**
Prep Time: **10** Minutes

Cook Time: **20** Minutes

Total Time: **30** Minutes

INGREDIENTS

- ½ lb. bok choy
- 1 tablespoon olive oil
- ½ red onion
- ¼ tsp salt
- 2 eggs
- 2 oz. cheddar cheese
- 1 garlic clove
- ¼ tsp dill

DIRECTIONS

1. In a bowl whisk eggs with salt and cheese
2. In a frying pan heat olive oil and pour egg mixture
3. Add remaining ingredients and mix well
4. Serve when ready

Serves: **2**

Prep Time: **10** Minutes

Cook Time: **20** Minutes

Total Time: **30** Minutes

INGREDIENTS

- 1 cup kale
- 1 tablespoon olive oil
- ½ red onion
- ¼ tsp salt
- 2 oz. cheddar cheese
- 1 garlic clove
- 2 eggs
- ¼ tsp dill

DIRECTIONS

1. In a bowl whisk eggs with salt and cheese
2. In a frying pan heat olive oil and pour egg mixture
3. Add remaining ingredients and mix well
4. Serve when ready

LEEK FRITATTA

Serves: **2**
Prep Time: **10** Minutes

Cook Time: **20** Minutes

Total Time: **30** Minutes

INGREDIENTS

- ½ cup leek
- 1 tablespoon olive oil
- ½ red onion
- 2 eggs
- ¼ tsp salt
- 2 oz. parmesan cheese
- 1 garlic clove
- ¼ tsp dill

DIRECTIONS

1. In a bowl whisk eggs with salt and cheese
2. In a frying pan heat olive oil and pour egg mixture
3. Add remaining ingredients and mix well
4. Serve when ready

BROCCOLI FRITATTA

Serves: **2**

Prep Time: **10**   Minutes

Cook Time: **20**   Minutes

Total Time: **30**   Minutes

INGREDIENTS

- 1 cup broccoli
- 1 tablespoon olive oil
- ½ red onion
- 2 eggs
- ¼ tsp salt
- 2 oz. cheddar cheese
- 1 garlic clove
- ¼ tsp dill

DIRECTIONS

1. In a bowl whisk eggs with salt and cheese
2. In a frying pan heat olive oil and pour egg mixture
3. Add remaining ingredients and mix well
4. Serve when ready

LEMON CHICKEN LEGS

Serves: **4**

Prep Time: **10** Minutes

Cook Time: **50** Minutes

Total Time: **60** Minutes

INGREDIENTS

- 4 chicken legs
- Juice from 1 lemon
- 2 tablespoons olive oil
- 1 tsp rosemary
- 1 tsp seasoning
- 2 garlic cloves
- 4-5 lemon slices

DIRECTIONS

1. In a bowl combine lemon juice, rosemary, olive oil, garlic gloves and seasoning
2. Toss the chicken with the marinade and let it marinade for 60 minutes
3. Place the chicken in a baking dish and 4-5 lemon slices along the chicken
4. Roast the chicken at 350 F for 40-50 minutes
5. When ready remove chicken from the oven and serve

CURRIED BEEF

Serves: **4**

Prep Time: **10** Minutes

Cook Time: **20** Minutes

Total Time: **30** Minutes

INGREDIENTS

- 1 lb. olive oil
- 1 lb. ground beef
- 1 garlic clove
- 2 tsp curry powder
- 1 tsp pepper
- 1 tsp salt

DIRECTIONS

1. In a skillet heat olive oil and sauté garlic until soft
2. Add the ground beef, pepper, curry powder and salt
3. When ready remove from heat and serve

SAUTEED SHRIMP

Serves: *4-*

Prep Time: *10*   Minutes

Cook Time: *20*   Minutes

Total Time: *30*   Minutes

INGREDIENTS

- 1 tsp olive oil
- 1 lb. shrimp
- 1 tablespoon herbes de Provence
- 1 tsp salt

DIRECTIONS

1. In a skillet heat olive oil
2. Add shrimp, herbes, salt and pepper
3. Cook the shrimp for 3-4 minutes per side
4. When ready remove to a plate and serve

Serves: **4-6**
Prep Time: **10**   Minutes

Cook Time: **8**   Hours

Total Time: **8**   Hours 10 Minutes

INGREDIENTS

- 2 lb. roast beef
- 1 cup beef broth
- 1 cup apple cider vinegar
- 1 tsp smoked paprika
- 1 tsp chili powder
- 1 tsp garlic powder
- 1 tsp cumin
- 1 tsp oregano

DIRECTIONS

1. In a bowl combine all spices together
2. Rub the beef with the mixture and let it marinade for 50-60 minutes
3. Place the beef into a slow cooker
4. Add broth, vinegar and cook on low for 7-8 hours
5. When ready remove from the cooker and serve

TURKEY BURGERS

Serves: *4*
Prep Time: *10* Minutes

Cook Time: *20* Minutes

Total Time: *30* Minutes

INGREDIENTS

- 1 lb. turkey
- 1 egg
- 1 tsp salt
- 1 tsp seasoning
- ½ cup red onion
- 1 tablespoon parsley

DIRECTIONS

1. Combine all ingredients together and mix well
2. Form 3-4 patties
3. In a skillet heat olive oil and cook each patty for 4-5 minutes per side
4. When ready remove from heat and serve

BROCCOLI CASSEROLE

Serves: **4**

Prep Time: **10** Minutes

Cook Time: **15** Minutes

Total Time: **25** Minutes

INGREDIENTS

- 1 onion
- 2 chicken breasts
- 2 tablespoons unsalted butter
- 2 eggs
- 2 cups cooked rice
- 2 cups cheese
- 1 cup parmesan cheese
- 2 cups cooked broccoli

DIRECTIONS

1. Sauté the veggies and set aside
2. Preheat the oven to 425 F
3. Transfer the sautéed veggies to a baking dish, add remaining ingredients to the baking dish
4. Mix well, add seasoning and place the dish in the oven
5. Bake for 12-15 minutes or until slightly brown
6. When ready remove from the oven and serve

BEAN FRITATTA

Serves: **2**
Prep Time: **10**   Minutes

Cook Time: **20**   Minutes

Total Time: **30**   Minutes

INGREDIENTS

- 1 cup black beans
- 1 tablespoon olive oil
- ½ red onion
- 2 eggs
- ¼ tsp salt
- 2 oz. cheddar cheese
- 1 garlic clove
- ¼ tsp dill

DIRECTIONS

1. In a bowl whisk eggs with salt and cheese
2. In a frying pan heat olive oil and pour egg mixture
3. Add remaining ingredients and mix well
4. Serve when ready

Serves: **3-4**

Prep Time: **10** Minutes

Cook Time: **20** Minutes

Total Time: **30** Minutes

INGREDIENTS

- 2 delicata squashes
- 2 tablespoons olive oil
- 1 tsp curry powder
- 1 tsp salt

DIRECTIONS

1. Preheat the oven to 400 F
2. Cut everything in half lengthwise
3. Toss everything with olive oil and place onto a prepared baking sheet
4. Roast for 18-20 minutes at 400 F or until golden brown
5. When ready remove from the oven and serve

CUCUMBER CHIPS

Serves: **2**

Prep Time: **10**   Minutes

Cook Time: **20**   Minutes

Total Time: **30**   Minutes

INGREDIENTS

- 1 lb. cucumber
- 1 tsp salt
- 1 tsp smoked paprika
- 1 tablespoon olive oil

DIRECTIONS

1. Preheat the oven to 425 F
2. In a bowl toss everything with olive oil and seasoning
3. Spread everything onto a prepared baking sheet
4. Bake for 8-10 minutes or until crisp
5. When ready remove from the oven and serve

SQUASH CHIPS

Serves: *2*
Prep Time: *10* Minutes

Cook Time: *20* Minutes

Total Time: *30* Minutes

INGREDIENTS

- 1 lb. squash
- 1 tsp salt
- 1 tsp smoked paprika
- 1 tablespoon olive oil

DIRECTIONS

1. Preheat the oven to 425 F
2. In a bowl toss everything with olive oil and seasoning
3. Spread everything onto a prepared baking sheet
4. Bake for 8-10 minutes or until crisp
5. When ready remove from the oven and serve

ZUCCHINI CHIPS

Serves: **2**

Prep Time: **10** Minutes

Cook Time: **20** Minutes

Total Time: **30** Minutes

INGREDIENTS

- 1 lb. zucchini
- 1 tsp salt
- 1 tsp smoked paprika
- 1 tablespoon olive oil

DIRECTIONS

1. Preheat the oven to 425 F
2. In a bowl toss everything with olive oil and seasoning
3. Spread everything onto a prepared baking sheet
4. Bake for 8-10 minutes or until crisp
5. When ready remove from the oven and serve

Serves: **2**
Prep Time: **10** Minutes

Cook Time: **20** Minutes

Total Time: **30** Minutes

INGREDIENTS

- 1 lb. potatoes
- 2 tablespoons olive oil
- 1 tablespoon smoked paprika
- 1 tablespoon salt

DIRECTIONS

1. Preheat the oven to 425 F
2. In a bowl toss everything with olive oil and seasoning
3. Spread everything onto a prepared baking sheet
4. Bake for 8-10 minutes or until crisp
5. When ready remove from the oven and serve

PIZZA

ZUCCHINI PIZZA

Serves: **6-8**
Prep Time: **10**   Minutes

Cook Time: **15**   Minutes

Total Time: **25**   Minutes

INGREDIENTS

- 1 pizza crust
- ½ cup tomato sauce
- ¼ black pepper
- 1 cup zucchini slices
- 1 cup mozzarella cheese
- 1 cup olives

DIRECTIONS

1. Spread tomato sauce on the pizza crust
2. Place all the toppings on the pizza crust
3. Bake the pizza at 425 F for 12-15 minutes
4. When ready remove pizza from the oven and serve

CAULIFLOWER PIZZA

Serves: **6-8**

Prep Time: **10**   Minutes

Cook Time: **15**   Minutes

Total Time: **25**   Minutes

INGREDIENTS

- 1 pizza crust
- 2 oz. parmesan cheese
- 1 tablespoon olive oil
- 4-5 basil leaves
- 1 cup mozzarella cheese
- 1 cup cauliflower

DIRECTIONS

1. Spread tomato sauce on the pizza crust
2. Place all the toppings on the pizza crust
3. Bake the pizza at 425 F for 12-15 minutes
4. When ready remove pizza from the oven and serve

Serves: **6-8**

Prep Time: **10** Minutes

Cook Time: **15** Minutes

Total Time: **25** Minutes

INGREDIENTS

- 1 pizza crust
- 1 garlic clove
- ½ lb. spinach
- ½ lb. soft cheese
- 2 oz. artichoke hearts
- 1 cup mozzarella cheese
- 1 tablespoon olive oil

DIRECTIONS

1. Spread tomato sauce on the pizza crust
2. Place all the toppings on the pizza crust
3. Bake the pizza at 425 F for 12-15 minutes
4. When ready remove pizza from the oven and serve

MINT PIZZA

Serves: **6-8**

Prep Time: **10**   Minutes

Cook Time: **15**   Minutes

Total Time: **25**   Minutes

INGREDIENTS

- 1 pizza crust
- 1 olive oil
- 1 garlic clove
- 1 cup mozzarella cheese
- 2 oz. mint
- 2 courgettes

DIRECTIONS

1. Spread tomato sauce on the pizza crust
2. Place all the toppings on the pizza crust
3. Bake the pizza at 425 F for 12-15 minutes
4. When ready remove pizza from the oven and serve

Serves: **6-8**
Prep Time: **10**   Minutes

Cook Time: **15**   Minutes

Total Time: **25**   Minutes

INGREDIENTS

- 2 pork sausages
- 1 tablespoon olive oil
- 2 garlic cloves
- 1 tsp fennel seeds
- ½ lb. ricotta
- 1 cup mozzarella cheese
- 1 oz. parmesan cheese
- 1 pizza crust

DIRECTIONS

1. Spread tomato sauce on the pizza crust
2. Place all the toppings on the pizza crust
3. Bake the pizza at 425 F for 12-15 minutes
4. When ready remove pizza from the oven and serve

Serves: **6-8**
Prep Time: **10**   Minutes

Cook Time: **15**   Minutes

Total Time: **25**   Minutes

INGREDIENTS

- 1 pizza crust
- 1 tablespoon olive oil
- 1 garlic clove
- 1 cup tomatoes
- 1 cup mozzarella cheese
- 1 carrot
- 1 cucumber

DIRECTIONS

1. Spread tomato sauce on the pizza crust
2. Place all the toppings on the pizza crust
3. Bake the pizza at 425 F for 12-15 minutes
4. When ready remove pizza from the oven and serve

SEVENTH COOKBOOK

ROASTED ALMONDS

Serves: **3-4**
Prep Time: **10**   Minutes

Cook Time: **20**   Minutes

Total Time: **30**   Minutes

INGREDIENTS

- 1 lb. almonds
- 2 tablespoons olive oil
- 1 tsp curry powder
- 1 tsp salt

DIRECTIONS

1. Preheat the oven to 400 F
2. Cut everything in half lengthwise
3. Toss everything with olive oil and place onto a prepared baking sheet
4. Roast for 18-20 minutes at 400 F or until golden brown
5. When ready remove from the oven and serve

ROASTED SQUASH

Serves: *3-4*

Prep Time: *10*   Minutes

Cook Time: *20*   Minutes

Total Time: *30*   Minutes

INGREDIENTS

- 2 delicata squashes
- 2 tablespoons olive oil
- 1 tsp curry powder
- 1 tsp salt

DIRECTIONS

1. Preheat the oven to 400 F
2. Cut everything in half lengthwise
3. Toss everything with olive oil and place onto a prepared baking sheet
4. Roast for 18-20 minutes at 400 F or until golden brown
5. When ready remove from the oven and serve

ZUCCHINI SOUP

Serves: **4**

Prep Time: **10**   Minutes

Cook Time: **20**   Minutes

Total Time: **30**   Minutes

INGREDIENTS

- 1 tablespoon olive oil
- 1 lb. zucchini
- ¼ red onion
- ½ cup all-purpose flour
- ¼ tsp salt
- ¼ tsp pepper
- 1 can vegetable broth
- 1 cup heavy cream

DIRECTIONS

1. In a saucepan heat olive oil and sauté zucchini until tender
2. Add remaining ingredients to the saucepan and bring to a boil
3. When all the vegetables are tender transfer to a blender and blend until smooth
4. Pour soup into bowls, garnish with parsley and serve

CHICKEN WITH CAULIFLOWER AND OLIVES

Serves: **4**

Prep Time: **10**   Minutes

Cook Time: **60**   Minutes

Total Time: **70**   Minutes

INGREDIENTS

- 1 bouquet thyme
- 1 head cauliflower
- ½ cup lemon juice
- 1 lb chicken breast
- 3 ½ tbs olive oil
- 1 ½ cup olives
- 4 cloves garlic
- 1 shallot
- 1 tsp salt
- 1 ½ tsp pepper
- ½ lemon zest

DIRECTIONS

1. Rinse the chicken breast and pat dry.
2. Spread the thyme springs in a baking dish.

3. Place the chicken over and add the cauliflower.
4. Mix the olive oil, olives, pepper, shallot, lemon juice and zest, garlic and salt.
5. Pour the mixture over the chicken.
6. Refrigerate overnight.
7. Bake at 400 for 1 hour.

ROSEMARY LEMON CHICKEN

Serves: *4*
Prep Time: *130*   Minutes
Cook Time: *20*   Minutes
Total Time: *150*   Minutes

INGREDIENTS

- 3 cloves garlic
- ½ cup lemon juice
- 1 tsp salt
- 3 tbs oil
- 1 lb chicken breast
- ½ cup rosemary

DIRECTIONS

1. Mix the lemon juice, oil, rosemary, salt and garlic.
2. Rinse the chicken breast and pat dry.
3. Place the chicken breast in a baking dish.
4. Pour the mixture over and refrigerate for 2-3 hours.
5. Grill the chicken for 6 minutes on each side.

SALMON BURGERS

Serves: **12**
Prep Time: **10**   Minutes

Cook Time: **30**   Minutes

Total Time: **40**   Minutes

INGREDIENTS

- 3 eggs
- 2 tbs flour
- ½ cup sesame seeds
- 4 tbs oil
- 2 tbs vinegar
- 2 cloves garlic
- 1 lb salmon
- 2 tsp ginger
- ½ cup scallions

DIRECTIONS

1. Rinse the salmon and pat dry.
2. Cut into cubes.
3. Mix the eggs, vinegar, scallions, 2 tbs oil, ginger, sesame seeds and ginger.
4. Add the salmon, then stir in the flour.
5. Form the mixture into patties.

6. Heat the rest of the oil in a frying pan.
7. Cook the patties for 5 minutes on each side.
8. Serve immediately.

Serves: **2**

Prep Time: **5**   Minutes

Cook Time: **5**   Minutes

Total Time: **10**   Minutes

INGREDIENTS

- ½ tsp salt
- 4 cucumbers
- 3 tbs oil
- 6 ounces argula
- 2 tbs lemon juice

DIRECTIONS

1. **Mix the ingredients in a large bowl.**
2. **Serve when ready**

TURKEY TACOS

Serves: **4**

Prep Time: **10** Minutes

Cook Time: **30** Minutes

Total Time: **40** Minutes

INGREDIENTS

- 1 ½ cups tomato puree
- 1 ½ tbs lime juice
- 1 ½ tsp oil
- 1 lb turkey
- 1 avocado
- 1 onion
- 1 red pepper
- 3 tsp chile powder
- 1 ½ tsp oregano
- ½ tsp garlic
- 2 tsp garlic
- 2 tsp cumin

DIRECTIONS

1. Mash the avocado, then add the lime juice and garlic and mix.
2. Heat the oil in a pan, then add the red pepper and onions and saute.

3. Add ground turkey.

4. Add the cumin, oregano, garlic and chile powder.

5. Add the tomato puree after the turkey is well cooked and simmer for a little.

6. Fill the lettuce cups with the meat mixture and serve.

AVOCADO BACON AND EGGS

Serves: **2**

Prep Time: **10** Minutes

Cook Time: **15** Minutes

Total Time: **25** Minutes

INGREDIENTS

- 2 eggs
- 2 tbs cheese
- 2 pieces bacon
- 1 avocado
- 1 tsp salt

DIRECTIONS

1. Preheat the oven to 425F.
2. Cut the avocado in half.
3. Scoop out some of the avocado.
4. Crack the egg inside the avocado.
5. Sprinkle some cheese and salt on top, then top with bacon.
6. Cook for 15 minutes.
7. Serve warm.

EGGS BAKED IN MUSHROOMS

Serves: **2**

Prep Time: **10** Minutes

Cook Time: **20** Minutes

Total Time: **30** Minutes

INGREDIENTS

- 4 mushrooms
- 1 tsp black pepper
- 4 eggs
- 3 tbs cheese
- 3 tbs parsley
- 1 tsp garlic powder
- 2 tbs oil
- 1 tsp salt

DIRECTIONS

1. Preheat the broiler.
2. Line a baking sheet.
3. Season the mushrooms with the oil, ½ tsp salt, ½ tsp pepper and ½ tsp garlic powder.
4. Broil for 5 minutes on each side.
5. Remove from oven then set the temperature to 400.
6. Crack an egg into each mushroom.

7. Sprinkle some cheese on top, then bake for 15 minutes.

8. Sprinkle with the remaining seasonings and garnish with parsley, then serve.

Serves: *4*
Prep Time: *10* Minutes

Cook Time: *20* Minutes

Total Time: *30* Minutes

INGREDIENTS

- 1 cauliflower
- 1 tsp black pepper
- 4 tbs oil
- 2 tsp turmeric
- 2 tsp salt
- 1 tsp garlic powder
- 2 tbs oregano

DIRECTIONS

1. Preheat the oven to 400F.
2. Chop the cauliflower.
3. Pour the oil over it.
4. Sprinkle the remaining ingredients over.
5. Bake for 20 minutes.

QUINOA SALAD

Serves: **4**

Prep Time: **10** Minutes

Cook Time: **20** Minutes

Total Time: **10** Minutes

INGREDIENTS

- 1 cup quinoa
- ½ cup cranberries
- 3 tsp olive oil
- ½ onion
- 1 bunch of kale
- 2 tsp salt
- 1 ½ tsp black pepper
- 1 cup feta
- ½ cup almonds
- 3 tsp lemon juice

DIRECTIONS

1. Cook the quinoa for 15 minutes in boiling salted water.
2. Drain in a sieve, then add the cranberries, cover and set aside.
3. Heat 1 ½ tsp oil and saute the onion.
4. Add the kale and cook for 5 minutes.
5. Season with salt.

6. Add the kale to quinoa, along with the feta and almonds and the lemon juice.

TURKEY MEATLOAF

Serves: **4**

Prep Time: **20** Minutes

Cook Time: **75** Minutes

Total Time: **95** Minutes

INGREDIENTS

- 1 egg
- 2 cups ketchup
- ½ cup bread crumbs
- 3 tbs soy sauce
- 2 ½ tsp basil
- 1 ½ tsp garlic powder
- ½ cup parsley
- 2 lb ground turkey
- ½ cup cheese
- 1 ½ tbs oregano
- 4 tbs Worcestershire sauce
- ½ cup oats

DIRECTIONS

1. Preheat the oven to 400F.
2. Mix together all of the ingredients until combined.

3. Form the mixture into a loaf shape.
4. Top with ketchup.
5. Bake for 75 minutes.

Serves: **4**
Prep Time: **20**   Minutes

Cook Time: **25**   Minutes

Total Time: **45**   Minutes

INGREDIENTS

- 1 ½ tsp vinegar
- 1 9-ounce can tomato sauce
- 8 hamburger buns
- 1 carrot
- 10 ounces ground beef
- 2 tsp garlic powder
- 1 ½ tsp chili powder
- ½ tsp black pepper
- ½ cup ketchup
- 1 tbs mustard
- 1 ½ tbs Worcestershire sauce
- 1 tbs tomato paste
- 1 cup onion

DIRECTIONS

1. **Preheat the broiler.**

2. Heat a skillet.

3. Great the carrot.

4. Cook the beef, carrot, and onion for 5 minutes.

5. Add the chili powder, garlic powder and pepper, then cook for another minute.

6. Mix the ketchup, mustard, Worcestershire sauce, vinegar, tomato pasta and tomato sauce.

7. Add the mixture to the skillet.

8. Simmer for 5 minutes.

9. Toast the halved buns.

10. Place the mixture on the bottom half of the bun, then cover with the top half.

SPINACH BALLS

Serves: **15**
Prep Time: **10** Minutes

Cook Time: **10** Minutes

Total Time: **20** Minutes

INGREDIENTS

- 1 ½ tbs butter
- 1 cup breadcrumbs
- 1 ½ tbs yogurt
- 2 tbs green onion
- 1 10-ounces package spinach
- 1 egg
- 1 tsp paprika
- 1 cup cheese

DIRECTIONS

1. Mix all of the ingredients in a bowl.
2. Form balls.
3. Bake at 350F for 15-20 minutes.

GREEN PESTO PASTA

Serves: **2**
Prep Time: **5** Minutes

Cook Time: **15** Minutes

Total Time: **20** Minutes

INGREDIENTS

- 4 oz. spaghetti
- 2 cups basil leaves
- 2 garlic cloves
- ¼ cup olive oil
- 2 tablespoons parmesan cheese
- ½ tsp black pepper

DIRECTIONS

1. Bring water to a boil and add pasta
2. In a blend add parmesan cheese, basil leaves, garlic and blend
3. Add olive oil, pepper and blend again
4. Pour pesto onto pasta and serve when ready

Serves: **2**

Prep Time: **5** Minutes

Cook Time: **5** Minutes

Total Time: **10** Minutes

INGREDIENTS

- 3 cups tomatoes
- 2 oz. mozzarella cheese
- 2 tablespoons basil
- 1 tablespoon olive oil

DIRECTIONS

1. In a bowl combine all ingredients together and mix well
2. Serve with dressing

Serves: 2
Prep Time: 5   Minutes

Cook Time: 5   Minutes

Total Time: 10   Minutes

INGREDIENTS

- 3 cups butternut squash
- 1 cup cooked couscous
- 2 cups kale leaves
- 2 tablespoons cranberries
- 2 oz. goat cheese
- 1 cup salad dressing

DIRECTIONS

1. In a bowl combine all ingredients together and mix well
2. Serve with dressing

Serves: **2**

Prep Time: **5**   Minutes

Cook Time: **5**   Minutes

Total Time: **10** Minutes

INGREDIENTS

- 2 hard boiled eggs
- ¼ cup red onion
- 2 tablespoons capers
- 1 tablespoon lime juice
- 3 oz. smoked salmon
- 1 tablespoon olive oil

DIRECTIONS

1. In a bowl combine all ingredients together and mix well
2. Serve with dressing

QUINOA SALAD

Serves:	**2**
Prep Time:	**5** Minutes
Cook Time:	**5** Minutes
Total Time:	**10** Minutes

INGREDIENTS

- 1 cup cooked quinoa
- 1 tablespoon olive oil
- 1 tablespoon mustard
- 2 tablespoons lemon juice
- 1 cucumber
- ½ red onion
- ½ cup almonds
- 1 tablespoon mint

DIRECTIONS

1. In a bowl combine all ingredients together and mix well
2. Serve with dressing

Serves: **2**

Prep Time: **5** Minutes

Cook Time: **5** Minutes

Total Time: **10** Minutes

INGREDIENTS

- 1 cup cucumber
- ¼ cup tomatoes
- ¼ cup red onion
- ¼ cup avocado
- ¼ cup feta cheese
- 1 tablespoon olives
- ¼ pecans
- 1 tablespoon vinegar
- 1 tsp olive oil

DIRECTIONS

1. In a bowl combine all ingredients together and mix well
2. Serve with dressing

AVOCADO SALAD

Serves: **2**

Prep Time: **5** Minutes

Cook Time: **5** Minutes

Total Time: **10** Minutes

INGREDIENTS

- 1 cup corn
- 1 cup tomatoes
- 1 cup cucumber
- ½ cup avocado
- ½ cup edamame
- 1 cup salad dressing

DIRECTIONS

1. In a bowl combine all ingredients together and mix well
2. Serve with dressing

BAKED LEMON SALMON

Serves: **1**

Prep Time: **10** Minutes

Cook Time: **20** Minutes

Total Time: **30** Minutes

INGREDIENTS

- 1 zucchini
- 1 onion
- 1 scallion
- 1 salmon fillet
- 1 tsp lemon zest
- 1 tsp olive oil
- Lemon slices

DIRECTIONS

1. Preheat the oven to 375 F
2. In a baking dish add zucchini, onion and sprinkle vegetables with salt and lemon zest
3. Lay salmon fillet and season with salt, lemon zest and olive oil
4. Bake at 375 F for 15-18 minutes
5. When ready remove from the oven and serve with lemon slices

MEDITERRANENA BUDDA BOWL

Serves: *1*

Prep Time: *10* Minutes

Cook Time: *10* Minutes

Total Time: *20* Minutes

INGREDIENTS

- 1 zucchini
- ¼ tsp oregano
- Salt
- 1 cup cooked quinoa
- 1 cup spinach
- 1 cup mixed greens
- ½ cup red pepper
- ¼ cup cucumber
- ¼ cup tomatoes
- parsley
- Tahini dressing

DIRECTIONS

1. In a skillet heat olive oil olive and sauté zucchini until soft and sprinkle oregano over zucchini
2. In a bowl add the rest of ingredients and toss to combine
3. Add fried zucchini and mix well

4. Pour over tahini dressing, mix well and serve

RUTABAGA HASH

Serves: **2**

Prep Time: **10**   Minutes

Cook Time: **20**   Minutes

Total Time: **30**   Minutes

INGREDIENTS

- 2 tablespoons olive oil
- 1 rutabaga
- ¼ cup onion
- ¼ cup red pepper
- 1 tsp salt
- ¼ tsp black pepper

DIRECTIONS

1. In a skillet heat olive oil and fry rutabaga for 3-4 minutes
2. Cook for another 5-6 minutes or until rutabaga is tender
3. Add onion, red pepper, black pepper, salt and stir to combine
4. Garnish with dill and serve

Serves: **4**

Prep Time: **10**   Minutes

Cook Time: **20**   Minutes

Total Time: **30**   Minutes

INGREDIENTS

- 1 tablespoon olive oil
- ¼ cup onion
- 2 stalks celery
- 1 garlic clove
- ¼ tsp coriander
- ¼ tsp cumin
- ¼ tsp turmeric
- ¼ tsp red pepper flakes
- 1 cauliflower
- 1 zucchini
- 2 tomatoes
- 1 tsp salt
- 1 cup vegetable broth
- 1 handful of baby spinach
- 1 tablespoon almonds
- 1 tablespoon cilantro

DIRECTIONS

1. In a skillet heat olive oil and sauté celery, garlic and onions for 4-5 minutes or until vegetables are tender

2. Add cumin, spices, coriander, cumin, turmeric red pepper flakes stir to combine and cook for another 1-2 minutes

3. Add zucchini, cauliflower, tomatoes, broth, spinach, water and simmer on low heat for 15-20 minutes

4. Add remaining ingredients and simmer for another 4-5 minutes

5. Garnish curry and serve

Serves: **2**
Prep Time: **5**   Minutes

Cook Time: **15** Minutes

Total Time: **20** Minutes

INGREDIENTS

- 1 cauliflower
- 1 tablespoon rosemary
- 1 cup vegetable stock
- 2 garlic cloves
- salt

DIRECTIONS

1. In a saucepan add cauliflower, stock and bring to a boil for 12-15 minutes
2. Blend cauliflower until smooth, add garlic, salt, rosemary and blend again
3. When ready pour in a bowl and serve

Serves: **2**

Prep Time: **10**   Minutes

Cook Time: **20**   Minutes

Total Time: **30**   Minutes

INGREDIENTS

- 1 tablespoon olive oil
- 2 shallots
- 2 cloves garlic
- 1 lb. brussels sprouts
- 1 cup vegetable stock
- 4 springs thyme
- ¼ cup pine nuts

DIRECTIONS

1. In a pan heat olive oil and cook shallots until tender
2. Add garlic, sprouts, thyme, stock and cook for another 4-5 minutes
3. Cover and cook for another 10-12 minutes or until sprouts are soft
4. When ready add pine nuts and serve

BREAD STUFFING

Serves: **4**

Prep Time: **10** Minutes

Cook Time: **25** Minutes

Total Time: **35** Minutes

INGREDIENTS

- One loaf candida diet bread
- 1 tablespoon olive oil
- ¼ cup celery
- ¼ cup onion
- ¼ cup mushrooms
- ¼ cup leeks
- 1 tsp thyme
- ¼ tsp salt
- 1 cup vegetable broth

DIRECTIONS

1. Cut a loaf of candida diet bread cubes and place cubes aside
2. In a skillet heat olive oil add onion, celery, mushrooms and sauté for 5-10 minutes
3. Season with thyme, pepper, salt and stir to combine
4. Add vegetable mixture, broth, bread cubes and stir to combine

5. Place stuffing mixture into a casserole dish and bake for 12-15 minutes
6. Bake until golden brown and serve

Serves: **2**
Prep Time: **10**   Minutes

Cook Time: **20**   Minutes

Total Time: **30**   Minutes

INGREDIENTS

- ¼ cup onion
- 1 clove garlic
- 1 lb. ground turkey
- 1 tsp all spice
- 1 tsp cumin
- 1 tsp salt
- 2 cups cabbage
- 1 tablespoon mint
- 1 red bell pepper
- Zest of 1 lemon
- 1 tablespoon lemon juice
- plain yogurt
- pint leaves

DIRECTIONS

1. In a skillet heat olive oil and sauté garlic, onion until soft

2. Add cumin, pepper, salt, all spice, ground turkey and sauté for 8-10 minutes

3. Add cabbage, red bell pepper, pint leaves, lemon zest and sauté for 4-5 minutes

4. When ready garnish with mint leaves, yogurt and serve

CAULIFLOWER FLORETS

Serves: **2**

Prep Time: **10** Minutes

Cook Time: **30** Minutes

Total Time: **40** Minutes

INGREDIENTS

- 2 tablespoons olive oil
- 1 lb. cauliflower florets
- 1 tsp apple cider vinegar
- 1 tsp paprika
- ¼ tsp salt
- ¼ tsp onion powder
- ¼ tsp garlic powder
- 1 stalk celery
- 1 scallion
- 1 tablespoon parsley
- ranch dressing

DIRECTIONS

1. In a bowl add salt, onion powder, garlic powder, paprika, apple cider vinegar, olive oil and whisk to combine
2. Add cauliflower florets to the bowl and toss to coat

3. Place florets on a prepared baking sheet and bake at 375 F for 25-30 minutes

4. When ready remove from the oven and transfer to a place

5. Garnish with scallion, celery, parsley, drizzle ranch dressing and serve

Serves: **8-12**

Prep Time: **10** Minutes

Cook Time: **20** Minutes

Total Time: **30** Minutes

INGREDIENTS

- 2 lb. steak
- 8-10 skewers
- Romain lettuce leaves
- Green onions

MARINADE

- ¼ cup coconut aminos
- 1 tablespoon water
- 1 tablespoon olive oil
- 2 cloves garlic
- 2 cloves onions
- 1 tablespoon sesame seeds
- 1 tsp pepper flakes

DIRECTIONS

1. Place all ingredients for the marinade in a bowl and mix well
2. Place steak cubes into the marinade bowl and let the meat marinade at least 8 hours

3. Preheat grill and place the steak kebabs on the grill
4. Cook for 4-5 minutes per side
5. When ready remove the kebabs from the gill and serve on lettuce leaves with green onions

IRISH STEW

Serves: **4**

Prep Time: **15** Minutes

Cook Time: **45** Minutes

Total Time: **60** Minutes

INGREDIENTS

- 4-5 slices bacon
- 2 lb. beef
- ¼ cup flour
- ½ tsp black pepper
- 4 carrots
- ½ cup beef broth

DIRECTIONS

1. Chop all ingredients in big chunks
2. In a large pot heat olive oil and add ingredients one by one
3. Cook for 5-6 or until slightly brown
4. Add remaining ingredients and cook until tender, 35-45 minutes
5. Season while stirring on low heat
6. When ready remove from heat and serve

CHICKPEA STEW

Serves: **4**
Prep Time: **15**   Minutes

Cook Time: **45**   Minutes

Total Time: **60**   Minutes

INGREDIENTS

- 2 garlic cloves
- 1 tablespoon olive oil
- 2 scallions
- 1 red bell pepper
- 1 tsp paprika
- 1 tsp cumin
- 3 cups chickpeas
- 3-4 mint leaves
- ½ cup white wine

DIRECTIONS

1. Chop all ingredients in big chunks
2. In a large pot heat olive oil and add ingredients one by one
3. Cook for 5-6 or until slightly brown
4. Add remaining ingredients and cook until tender, 35-45 minutes
5. Season while stirring on low heat

6. When ready remove from heat and serve

CASSEROLE RECIPES

BACON CASSEROLE

Serves: **4**

Prep Time: **10** Minutes

Cook Time: **15** Minutes

Total Time: **25** Minutes

INGREDIENTS

- 4-5 slices bacon
- 3-4 tablespoons butter
- 5-6 tablespoons flour
- 2 cups milk
- 3 cups cheddar cheese
- 2 cups chicken breast
- 1 tsp seasoning mix

DIRECTIONS

1. Sauté the veggies and set aside
2. Preheat the oven to 425 F
3. Transfer the sautéed veggies to a baking dish, add remaining ingredients to the baking dish
4. Mix well, add seasoning and place the dish in the oven
5. Bake for 12-15 minutes or until slightly brown

6. When ready remove from the oven and serve

Serves: **4**
Prep Time: **10**   Minutes

Cook Time: **25**   Minutes

Total Time: **35**   Minutes

INGREDIENTS

- 1 tablespoon olive oil
- 1 red onion
- 1 bell pepper
- 2 cloves garlic
- 1 can black beans
- 1 cup chicken
- 1 can green chilis
- 1 can enchilada sauce
- 1 cup cheddar cheese
- 1 cup sour cream

DIRECTIONS

1. Sauté the veggies and set aside
2. Preheat the oven to 425 F
3. Transfer the sautéed veggies to a baking dish, add remaining ingredients to the baking dish
4. Mix well, add seasoning and place the dish in the oven

5. Bake for 15-25 minutes or until slightly brown
6. When ready remove from the oven and serve

MEXICAN PIZZA

Serves: **4**

Prep Time: **10**   Minutes

Cook Time: **20**   Minutes

Total Time: **30**   Minutes

INGREDIENTS
Pizza
- 1 ½ tsp cumin
- ½ tsp cayenne pepper
- 2 15-ounce cans black beans
- 8 corn tortillas
- 1 15-ounces can olives
- 3 tsp paprika
- 1 bell pepper
- 1 bunch green onions
- 1 cup cheese
- 1 red onion
- 4 tomatoes

DIRECTIONS

1. Preheat the oven to 400F.
2. Bake the tortillas until crispy.

3. Heat the black beans, cumin, paprika, and cayenne until smooth.
4. Divide the bean among the tortillas, then spread evenly.
5. Top with the onion, bell pepper, olives and tomatoes.
6. Sprinkle the cheese on top.
7. Bake for 10 minutes.

CHICKEN PIZZA

Serves: **4**

Prep Time: **10** Minutes

Cook Time: **20** Minutes

Total Time: **30** Minutes

INGREDIENTS

- 1 ½ tbs basil
- 1 cup pizza sauce
- 6 chicken strips
- 1 10-ounces garlic bread
- 1 ½ cup cheese

DIRECTIONS

1. Preheat the oven to 400F.
2. Place the garlic bread on a baking sheet.
3. Bake for 10 minutes, then spread the sauce over.
4. Cut the chicken strips and arrange over.
5. Sprinkle with cheese and basil.
6. Bake until the cheese melts.

CASSEROLE PIZZA

Serves: *6-8*

Prep Time: *10*   Minutes

Cook Time: *15*   Minutes

Total Time: *25*   Minutes

INGREDIENTS

- 1 pizza crust
- ½ cup tomato sauce
- ¼ black pepper
- 1 cup zucchini slices
- 1 cup mozzarella cheese
- 1 cup olives

DIRECTIONS

1. Spread tomato sauce on the pizza crust
2. Place all the toppings on the pizza crust
3. Bake the pizza at 425 F for 12-15 minutes
4. When ready remove pizza from the oven and serve

ZUCCHINI PIZZA

Serves: **6**

Prep Time: **25** Minutes

Cook Time: **15** Minutes

Total Time: **40** Minutes

INGREDIENTS

- 20 slices pepperoni
- 2 tsp herb seasoning
- 4 zucchinis
- 1 ½ tsp salt
- 1 lb mozzarella

DIRECTIONS

1. Preheat the broiler.
2. Wash the zucchinis and cut off the ends.
3. Cut into even slices.
4. Spray a baking dish with non-stick spray.
5. Place the zucchini slices on the baking sheet.
6. Sprinkle with the salt and the herbs.
7. Cover with the grated cheese.
8. Broil until the cheese is starting to melt.
9. Place the pepperoni slices on top.
10. Broil for another 5 minutes, remove and serve

THANK YOU FOR READING THIS BOOK!